ANINE KRIEGLER is a researcher wi

at the University of Cape Town. She

both UCT and Cambridge University, and is a doctoral candidate in Criminology. Her research interests include the measurement of crime and victimisation, and drug markets.

MARK SHAW is the Director of the Centre of Criminology. He holds the NRF Chair in African Justice and Security and is the Director of the Global Initiative against Transnational Organized Crime, Geneva. He worked for 12 years at the United Nations Office on Drugs and Crime (UNODC). His research focuses on illicit markets and organised crime.

A Citizen's Guide to Crime Trends in South Africa

Anine Kriegler and Mark Shaw

Jonathan Ball Publishers

Johannesburg and Cape Town

Published in South Africa in 2016 by
JONATHAN BALL PUBLISHERS
A division of Media24 Limited
PO Box 33977
Jeppestown
2043

ISBN 978-1-86842-722-2
ebook ISBN 978-1-86842-723-9

Every effort has been made to trace the copyright holders
and to obtain their permission for the use of copyright
material. The publishers apologise for any errors or
omissions and would be grateful to be notified of any
corrections that should be incorporated in future editions
of this book.

Twitter: www.twitter.com/JonathanBallPub
Facebook: www.facebook.com/JonathanBallPublishers
Blog: http://jonathanball.bookslive.co.za/

Cover: National Police Commissioner Bheki Cele and other
members of the SAPS at the crime scene, where British
tourist Anni Dewani's body was found in Khayelitsha,
18 November 2010 (Gallo Images/Sowetan/Elvis ka Nyelenzi)

Cover by Michiel Botha
Design and typesetting by Triple M Design, Johannesburg
Printed and bound by CREDA Communications, Cape Town
Set in 10.75pt/18pt Melior LT Std

Contents

Preface and acknowledgements

This book is the outcome of an attempt to respond to media queries on the annual release of crime statistics in South Africa. In 2015, the Centre of Criminology at the University of Cape Town produced a short descriptive guide to assist journalists and others who wanted to understand the problems with the SAPS crime statistics release in September and to place it in longer perspective. We are grateful to Barry Bateman, with whom we discussed it, and to Chris de Kock, who partnered on that initial product. However, we wanted something that provided not an overview of the data but started to show how the numbers themselves might help determine what must be done to reduce violent crime. This book is the result.

We are extremely grateful to our colleagues and students at the Centre of Criminology and the Safety and Violence

Initiative for ideas, debates and discussions about different parts of the argument. A seminar in late 2015 provided some indication of the importance of the long-term analysis of murder data. Social media comments on an article we published in the *Daily Maverick* on homicide trends also proved to be a spur to more in-depth thinking about what the data might say about policy options. We must also thank Jeremy Boraine of Jonathan Ball Publishers for his enthusiasm for publishing a work that we believe is in the public interest.

This work is based on the research supported by the South African Research Chairs Initiative of the Department of Science and Technology and the National Research Foundation of South Africa (Grant No 47303). Any opinion, finding and conclusion or recommendation expressed in this material is that of the authors and the NRF does not accept any liability in this regard. Anine is also supported in her research by the David and Elaine Potter Foundation.

Mark is grateful for his family's usual forbearance. Thanks, finally, from Anine to Thomas van Heerden for doing everything that wasn't this.

As we were completing this book, in March 2016, Cape Town was rocked by the brutal murders of two teenage girls. Sixteen-year-old Franziska Blöchliger and nineteen-year-old Sinoxolo Mafevuka were killed about a week apart. One was found hours after being separated from her family during a run in Tokai Forest and the other was found at sunrise in a communal toilet in Khayelitsha. More than the similarity, what struck many was the contrast in how the cases were received by the police and the public. What was reignited was a debate – arguably *the* chronic South African debate – about the distribution and meaning of violence within pervasive systems of privilege, exclusion and fear. Addressing the problem of crime will inevitably require addressing those issues. It will also require that we all take the responsibility to inform ourselves about the nature of what we're talking about. We are conscious that our work around crime data is about real human beings and their experiences. It is for that reason that this book is dedicated to Franziska and Sinoxolo.

Introduction

South Africans care a lot about crime. We think and worry about it, plan and insure against it, develop and share theories about it, report on and read about it, and talk about it ... a lot. Crime is by no means a middle class and/or white preserve, but cuts across race and class, with black and poor people in fact disproportionately affected by crime (especially violent crime)[1] and by fear of it.[2] We are not the only country concerned with crime, but our high crime rates combine with other national anxieties – around race, social change, cohesion, history, and so on – to form a cocktail of issues that is potent and uniquely our own. We also find ourselves in the unusual and unenviable position of having both high crime levels and relatively good statistical reach and capacity. There are many who criticise what has been called our obsession with crime, and the ways in which it shapes our priorities, relationships, spaces and collective identity.

Without downplaying such cautions about the primacy of beliefs about crime in our national conception of self – quite the contrary – this book takes the view that our concern with crime is neither avoidable nor undesirable. The conversations about crime that happen in the press, on social media, in houses of every size throughout the country, in neighbourhood watch meetings, boardrooms, break rooms, bars, streets, queues and every other place we come together are an inevitable result of the place crime occupies in our social and political lives. More important, such conversations are an important arena of connection and contestation. Crime, its measurement and its control are not technocratic issues best left to those with specialised education and experience, and at ease with quantitative methods, people perhaps imagined as above the sometimes petty, sometimes downright ugly emotional fray of grappling with crime in this country. It simply doesn't (or shouldn't) take degrees in statistics, criminology or history to get a decent grasp on just what we should make of the figures and graphs that the South African Police Service (SAPS) currently produces on an annual basis for public consumption.

At the same time, we all share a responsibility to ground ourselves in reality. There is and always will be a lot about crime that remains open to interpretation and discussion, and scope for our personal and political worldviews to play out. But there are a few things that we should all be reasonably able to agree on, so that we don't talk past each other or waste time trying to understand or solve problems that aren't the ones that need to be understood or solved. Failing to engage with these issues impoverishes the quality of our discourse on every level, and makes it more difficult to make any progress. Besides the obvious – that crime enacts harm on those it touches – there are at least four major reasons why we should all continue to engage each other and ourselves in thinking about the magnitude and nature of crime, and why we should attempt to do so with some basic understanding of what we're actually talking about: crime is expensive; knowledge in the form of figures can be especially beguiling; crime is unavoidably political; and finally, as this book aims to show, crime can tell us things about our society that we might otherwise miss or misunderstand.

Crime is costly

Driven in part by a growing focus on maximising fiscal 'bang for buck', the last three decades have seen the proliferation of attempts to measure and compare the costs of crime and crime control. The direct costs are relatively easy to compute. The 2016/2017 national budget allocated R87.5 billion for police services and R41.7 billion for law courts and prisons, for a combined R129.2 billion.[3] That's about 10 cents in every rand of government expenditure allocated in a tight budget, at a time when global economic pressure is high and local political consensus around appropriate state spending is low. In addition, turnover in the private security industry is said to be in the region of about R60 billion a year.[4] So the direct annual costs of attempting to prevent and respond to crime in this country are around R189 billion.

Those costs buy the services of, and facilities used by, 194 000 SAPS employees,[5] 487 000 private security officers,[6] about 40 000 Correctional Services staff[7] and about 22 000 Justice department staff.[8] Thus the jobs of about three-quarters of a million people in this country are, at least to some extent, influenced by what the crime statistics tell us and how we interpret and respond to them. This is because the statistics are one of the most basic tools for understanding and quantifying our crime problem – how much of it there is, what shapes it takes in different places, and therefore where and how we should allocate resources to do something about it.

But the costs of crime go far beyond these direct financial allocations. There are the costs of the property damaged and lost, costs related to insurance, to securing homes and property, to dealing with the medical results of crime both in the short term (for example, treating injuries following assault and providing antiretrovirals for rape survivors) and the long term (for example, treating crime-related disability and trauma), and so on. A study in 2000 estimated that the direct medical costs and loss of income alone cost a survivor of rape R1 605 and a survivor of attempted murder R3 928.[9] Other research estimated that each homicide victim in the Western Cape in 1998 involved productivity and opportunity costs of about R88 000.[10] One attempt at including direct financial losses, as well as medical, emotional, institutional and private security costs, estimated that the aggregated cost of crime in South Africa amounted to 7.8 per cent of GDP in 2007.[11] Cable theft alone has been estimated to cost the country R5 billion a year.[12]

Crime diverts human, financial and time resources in the state, business and individual spheres away from more productive investments in development and growth.[13] The cumulative lost growth due to crime is hard to estimate, not least because of the challenge of capturing the lost benefits of spending on other things, that is, the opportunity costs. One rand spent on policing is one rand not spent on education or public transport; a productive worker who emigrates out of fear of crime is one who ceases to contribute to the local economy; a month spent on compassionate leave following a serious crime is a month not spent working; equally, a month in prison for a healthy young person represents a lifetime of reduced prospects of earning a salary to help their family; and on and on. Crime also disproportionately affects those to whom it is most devastating: the poor. Those who have very little are the least able to protect themselves from being robbed of it, and lack the insurance or resources to recover from the shock, thereby worsening cycles of poverty and entrenching inequality.

Methods of estimating the economic impact of crime have improved in nuance and sophistication over the years, for example extending to use self-reported offending rather than just official records, and attempting to account for the cumulative costs that criminal justice action can exert on already marginalised communities. These methods will no doubt continue to improve. But quantitative approaches will always be beset by debates about the appropriate weighting of costs of various kinds and against different groups in society, about whether some crucial factors can be meaningfully translated into monetary terms, and about how to take account of inevitably differing conceptions of fairness and equity. These questions are by no means only of local concern. Quantifying, comparing and setting targets so as to mitigate the impact of crime on people's livelihoods and lives is no simple task. One of the United Nations' Sustainable Development Goals, adopted in September 2015, is the promotion of just, peaceful and inclusive socities, and debate is ongoing around the issue of how to measure security as a component of human development. Whether neatly quantified or not, crime and how we respond to it manifestly have considerable impact on the livelihoods not just of victims, perpetrators and law enforcement personnel, but also of the entire society. Crime critically obstructs urgent efforts to improve national wellbeing.

Crime statistics are powerful but beguiling

Figures of all kinds have weight in how we think about our world. When we wish to know about and describe places, we often turn to the collective numbers associated with them, such as their population, aggregate wealth, unemployment rate and crime rate. But this is a fairly new way of approaching things. It was only really in the late eighteenth and early nineteenth centuries in Europe and America that there came to be sufficient capacity for, and perceived value in, neatly categorising and counting various things about the individuals in a society.[14] From about the 1830s, ever-larger volumes of numerical information came to be produced and used in the governance of people and places, helping to consolidate these into conceptual and practical bureaucratic units.[15] Quantifying rates of deviancy – of illness, madness and criminality – was central to this process from the first, with statistical description increasingly taking the place of causal arguments involving human nature or the supernatural.[16] In other words, where once crime may have been primarily understood as the outcome of the universal and individual struggle between good and evil, it came to be thought that there was a certain proportion of society that was dangerous, and that this proportion allowed for and required identification, measurement, ideally prediction and certainly management.[17]

This is a simple but important historical point: crime statistics exist because they are thought to be useful. Collecting, compiling and interpreting them uses limited resources of money and time. The expense makes sense only if it is believed that having the resulting information can help give rise to better understanding and better decisions. As the United Nations manual on crime statistics puts it, statistics can be a partial but invaluable tool to 'help Governments to assess and monitor the conditions, circumstances and trends of well-being and the social impact of public expenditures and policies'.[18] Statistics influence decisions about which areas should be allocated more police, what crimes should be targeted for reduction, which police station managers are doing well or badly and whether the police, courts and communities in general are doing the right things to combat and respond to crime. The crime statistics influence decisions about how those who enforce order should conceive of and conduct themselves in relation to the rest of society – for example, whether they should call themselves generals or commissioners – and when they should be allowed or encouraged to use deadly force.[19]

The annual peak in popular interest around the release of the South African crime statistics, at least in the press and on social media, suggests that many ordinary people also consider them worthy of some form of attention. Although some people are highly suspicious of the validity of the statistics as they are presented by the SAPS, or by the poverty of the numbers in fully capturing the messy and painful personal realities of crime, few seem to question whether the task is meaningful or worthwhile at all. The outcry around the moratorium on the release of crime statistics in 2000 may well have been in large part expressive just of frustration and suspicion, but it was bolstered by a sense that we were worse off without that knowledge. There appears to be a general popular sense that, whether or not the numbers we have tell the story we want to hear or are of good enough quality, there is some point in having them. On the basis of our understanding of crime, which may well be partly informed by our understanding of crime statistics (although likely less so than by our own experiences, what we hear from peers and the media, and our other beliefs about ourselves and society), we may change our route home, our mode of transportation, our children's curfew, our insurance profile, our purchases, our hiring practices, our neighbourhood, our vote, and so on.

This presents two related problems. First, statistics can be selected and manipulated with varying degrees of subtlety, and are often used not to test assumptions or teach new things but instead to give a sense of reality to what people already feel or want to prove. People tend to believe that the information that fits with and confirms the rest of their views is true, and that the information that does not suit them is false.[20] So it is common to see people embrace and share those crime figures that suggest that the country's safety situation is deteriorating, and in the same breath reject a figure that suggests the contrary as being the product of police machination. Because they seem so important and concrete, but are inevitably incomplete and sometimes downright ambiguous, crime statistics here and everywhere are a 'spinner's paradise', easily prodded and shaped to 'prove' just about anything.[21]

The second problem is that many people are intimidated by anything that looks like mathematics, have limited confidence and skill in telling good quantitative work from bad, and are inclined to consider any argument accompanied by numbers, percentages, probabilities and graphs a better one than an argument without. An infographic can speak a thousand words, regardless of whether those words are accurate or worthwhile. Even statistics created with all the goodwill in the world may be of poor quality, as is arguably the case with many about the developing world.[22] Numbers can make complex and ambiguous things seem simple and concrete, even as their production introduces new domains of uncertainty.[23] This means that crime statistics are fraught with the potential for both conscious and unconscious deception of ourselves and others, with the result that the decisions they inform may be very poor. This situation is made especially frustrating by the fact that crime statistics are not themselves very complicated at all. They can be used and combined with other information in interesting and skilful ways, and they can serve as subtle social and political tools, but people with even a low level of numeracy should be able to grasp their essential features and begin to use them to make sense of and change their world.

Even more frustrating is the fact that the people of South Africa are not just the subject matter of this information, *but its primary data gatherers*. Most of the figures we have about crime are created bit by bit every day, when individuals make the choice to pick up the phone or walk through the doors of one of the country's about 1 130 police stations and take the time to report on what they've experienced, what they know and what they need. For the most part, the role of the police or other researchers in creating the crime statistics is just to take this information as (largely) voluntarily provided by the public, categorise and add it up, and combine it with some other information to make it easier to interpret. The information is for the most part given in order to elicit direct action wherever possible,[24] but based on the interest and sometimes incredulity with which the annual release of the statistics is met, it seems reasonable to conclude that there is also a genuine expectation that it will be usefully returned. That mass of information is not given or surrendered for the police or others to dispose of how they please; it is loaned with the understanding that it will be returned in a format that makes it possible for everyone to understand what is happening in terms of crime and what is being done about it.

Crime statistics do not belong to the South African Police Service, the government, a handful of academics or other specialists, and/or the press. They are public property, and the public have a right to access and understand them. No party has the right to try to package or dole them out so as to avoid causing panic or receiving criticism. Moreover, no party should be able to do so. Every individual should be able to take up the crime statistics and use them to help draw conclusions and make decisions about their lives.

Crime is political

It can be tempting, when faced with the undeniable realities of crime, to imagine that crime is a simple fact, an easily identified thing that objectively happens and can be counted in the same way that we may count atoms or cell divisions. But this is seldom the case with social phenomena. Social events are made meaningful by their contexts. Each is embedded in, and followed by, a process of negotiation and interpretation that determines how we think and feel about and react to it. For example, the act of presenting a bouquet of flowers to another person means entirely different things in different contexts – in a romantic relationship, at a funeral, from an employer to an employee, from a child to a parent, from a motorist to the traffic cop planning to write them a speeding fine, and so on – to say nothing of the variations between different cultural contexts and different eras. The meaning of an ostensibly simple act, such as transferring flowers from one person's hands to another's, only begins to make sense in that it invokes a whole complex world of norms, assumptions and relationships.

In the case of crime, the process of making meaning may seem relatively simple; we have a codified system of laws according to which we can evaluate the act in question. However complex the issue may be, it should be possible for sufficiently skilled and experienced people to come to a defensible determination of whether or not a crime has been committed. Therefore, it should be feasible to count up those crimes and use that count to draw meaningful conclusions about crime. In a minimal sense, this is so.

Even in its letter, however, the law is itself a product of history, more or less democratic processes, inertia and negotiation and conflict between various pressures and interest groups. The case of apartheid laws makes this especially clear in the South African context. It likely strikes most young South Africans as inconceivable and absurd that until 1985 it was deemed appropriate to identify marriage or extramarital sexual relationships between people of different officially classified races as a distinct phenomenon, a problem deserving of government attention, and an appropriate subject of criminal law and punishment. Conversely, it might not that long ago have struck many people as surprising that, as of 2007, it is legally possible for a man in South Africa to be raped by a woman. The list of substances considered illegal or controlled changes from time to time. There are laws now to control items or activities that didn't even exist two or three decades ago. Legal days and hours for the sale of alcohol have in recent years changed a number of times in some places, and will no doubt continue to do so as political pressures and alliances shift.

The law undergoes changes large and small on a constant basis. The process of change can be slow or it can happen in sudden bursts. Despite the ideal of public participation, the law can seem technical and remote from ordinary people, a matter of impenetrable jargon being crafted in parliamentary meeting rooms and judges' chambers. But whether through active legal challenge, lobbying, electoral politics or the expression and development of the amorphous arena of public opinion, the law takes its shape from its society. When we count crimes, even according to careful and explicit legal definitions, the very system of definition and counting we use is a complicated product of our collective historical and present values, priorities and structures.

When it comes to the reach and application of the law, the role of these pervasive social factors becomes even clearer. Even for

13

what may seem like relatively clear-cut crimes, such as theft or assault, there are a number of incidents that may never register with those involved or who observe them as criminal, never mind reach the attention of law enforcement. We tend not to see the behaviour of those similar to us and close to us through a criminal lens.[25] When we're out having drinks and a friend removes cash from our wallet despite it being their turn to buy a round, and they push and swear at us in the course of the ensuing argument, we may well feel angry or betrayed, but it may never occur to us or anyone else around that we have been victims of and witnesses to theft, assault and crimen injuria. Were the circumstances, characters and relationships involved even slightly different, these actions would be reported, registered as crimes, and might result in a trial and potential conviction and sentence. Even in the courts, where every effort is made to standardise and depersonalise decision-making, research shows that whether someone is deemed a criminal and how it is deemed that the state should respond are influenced by such ostensibly irrelevant factors as the race, gender and age of the parties involved.[26] Like its content, the application of law is determined by the shapes of our social structures and patterns of power. These are subject to change.

Further, the outcomes of these processes feed back into the shape of our society. Crime and fear of crime change our behaviour and our spaces in profound ways. More than two-thirds of South Africans feel unsafe walking alone in their area when it is dark,[27] and although the evidence locally is less clear,[28] it is generally women, old people and ethnic minorities who are disproportionately affected by this fear, which constrains their behaviour as a result.[29] Our experiences and feelings about crime change the shapes of our homes, streets, businesses and cities.[30] In turn, the shapes of our spaces and the ways in which we distribute resources over the long, medium and short term determine who experiences what crimes and to some extent what the impact of those crimes will be. The people we label as criminal carry and enact the consequences of that label for the rest of their lives.[31] As typified by ongoing debates about the magnitude and salience of the problems of farm killings or crimes committed by foreigners, the prevalence and patterns of crime infuse our political discourse and our beliefs about rights, race, nationhood and the legitimacy of our leaders. Beliefs about levels of lawlessness are made to stand in for the success, value and prospects of the entire post-apartheid democratic project.[32]

Not only is crime embedded in our broader ideas about ourselves and each other, but it also shapes these ideas. As such, crime can never be a matter just for legal and law enforcement professionals. It is inextricably linked with how we live our lives, how we think lives should be lived, and who gets to make and enforce those decisions.

• • •

These are some of the reasons why it's important not to leave the question of crime and its measurement to the bureaucrats and technocrats, and instead to involve ourselves consciously in their unavoidable politics. We should do so responsibly, if we care at all about making good decisions for ourselves and our society. This means being honest and informed in our relationship with the evidence. In crime, as in all else, we all have a great many ideas about the world that we think of as 'facts', but which are simply not supported by any rigorous investigation of reality.

In response to the 2015 release of the crime statistics, the key political actors made a range of claims with varying degrees of reasonableness, but almost none with any obvious basis beyond conjecture. During the parliamentary portfolio committee briefing on the crime statistics, both the Police minister and the National Police Commissioner stressed that the figures should be seen as reflecting primarily the social circumstances the police and nation are faced with rather than police performance, and also that the statistics presented were accurate and methodologically sound. The African National Congress (ANC) statement reaffirmed its 'confidence in the quality and credibility of these statistics', and noted with concern the 'slight' and 'marginal' increases in some crime types, as well as the 'significant and commendable achievements' evidenced in the trends in other crimes.[33] The Police and Prisons Civil Rights Union suggested that it was impossible to draw 'mathematical conclusions' or 'discredit individuals' on the basis of the crime statistics, and criticised those who failed adequately to take account of the fact that 'policing in South Africa is relatively new and its approach cannot be ignorant to the current South African realities'.[34]

On the other hand, the Inkatha Freedom Party registered its disappointment with the release because the statistics were 'disconnected from the current crime reality' in the country, as there had been a 'spiralling crime rate' in the six months between the reporting year-end in March 2015 and the release at the end of September.[35] The grounds on which this conclusion was reached were not specified. The Freedom Front Plus announced that the statistics indicated that 'South Africa is increasingly becoming a violent country', and went on to say that 'the credibility of the statistics is also suspect', a claim apparently based on complaints from 'many people' as well as the chief spokesperson's personal experience in reporting a crime.[36] The Democratic Alliance (DA) claimed that the murder rate was 'what one would expect from a country at war'.[37] Trade union Solidarity was adamant that the increase in serious crime 'should be laid at the door of a leaderless police service that failed to combat crime'.[38]

In the course of two or three days, the crime statistics were confidently described by the various parties as accurate and as entirely inaccurate, as showing positive signs and as showing disastrous signs, and as saying good things, bad things or nothing at all about police performance. In many cases the same people made apparently contradictory claims within the same statement or even paragraph. Social media, the comments sections of major news websites and informal conversation reflect many of these same positions, perhaps in cruder terms but usually with much the same evidentiary basis. The same thing happens every year, regardless of what the figures look like. We should do better, and we can.

Sifting through such competing claims about what the crime statistics are, and what they mean, needn't be a matter of simply trusting the familiar voices and the ideologically aligned. So this book aims foremost to empower ordinary people in South Africa to sift through the noise and have better, more informed and productive conversations about the crime statistics. Having raised these issues and provided some information on how it might be useful to approach them, it does not follow that we will all agree or come to the same conclusions about them. Many questions about crime, its measurement and what should be done about it have been asked for as long as some concept of criminal deviance has existed. They are and should rightly be asked every day by experts and law enforcement officials and activists and politicians and religious leaders and everyone else who cares to. There is also a great deal about crime that the statistics alone can't answer. Still, it is our view that a broad understanding of how this particular pool of numerical knowledge works and what it looks like can help us to ask the right questions, so that we don't waste precious resources of time, money and attention trying continually to untangle the wrong knots with one hand tied behind our backs.

This book also derives from the belief that crime and criminal justice statistics, when combined with other forms and sources of knowledge and solid expert analysis, can be tools not just for better thinking and decision-making, but also for accountability. There is so much more knowledge about crime buried in the figures than just the percentage by which a particular crime type went up or down in the country in the last year. Some of it is contained in the relevant agencies' annual reports, which, unlike the 'crime statistics', tend not to enjoy much public attention and interrogation. But the quality and accessibility of this knowledge determines its power to promote participation, transparency and responsiveness in the collective efforts to address one of the problems that most concerns the people of South Africa. Although the figures are imperfect, meaningful access to such figures may help contribute to the effectiveness and commitment to justice of those to whom we officially entrust it.[39]

Finally, this book seeks to show not so much what the statistics say as how they can help us understand our social world. This is the fourth major reason why it is important that we keep engaging with the issue of crime with the strongest possible commitment to honesty and rigour. The questions of how much crime we have compared to other places and times, of which crimes are happening where and to whom, of what it is that people do after they experience a crime, and of how these factors shift over time can tell us something important about the kind of society we are and are creating. The crime statistics are certainly flawed, and there is a risk in placing too much stock in them as *the* indicator of national health, but if used with care they can be a valuable social barometer on both the macro and micro levels.[40] This is an important first step to crafting effective responses.

So we begin by reviewing how the figures are made, what they definitely can't do and why we need to be very careful in how we use and interpret them. Key to this is an understanding of the imperfection of all our sources of knowledge about crime, of the challenges raised by the fact that we hold the same people responsible for both the content and the accuracy of the figures, of the particular complications in the South African historical context, and of the ways in which we can try to mitigate some of these problems.

Having taken proper account of the bathwater, we can then attend to the baby. The first big question that most people will want answered about crime is how much of it there is compared to other places. We unpack what the official statistics can tell us about the widely held belief that South Africa is the crime capital of the world, a consideration that profoundly informs many South Africans' sense of the legitimacy of our political and security order, and indeed whether they wish to remain a part of it. For all that they may be politically weighty and interesting, however, simply stating the national numbers or ranks tells us very little of practical use. What they can do is help illuminate what it is about countries that determines where they find themselves in those rankings. We can make some progress towards understanding why crime happens simply by knowing where in the world it disproportionately does.

But when it comes to the situation of crime as it actually

touches people's lives, the national picture is not only a clumsy abstraction, but in fact also obscures far more than it reveals. Turning the crime statistics into something that might help individuals and communities make appropriate decisions requires reducing them to the smallest possible spatial and social scale. There is an enormous range of experiences of crime within the country, within each city, each neighbourhood and each household. Failure to grasp how the national crime picture breaks down on the individual level is part of what makes it possible for there to be such a profound disconnection between real risks, perceptions and fear. We have no hope of useful progress against crime if we don't know where in the country it is happening and to whom.

Another problem with how we usually consume the crime statistics is that we have a tendency to gloss over the details of the past with vague, broad brushstrokes that may be completely wrong. The question of whether the country is more dangerous now than ever in living memory is another key consideration in many people's assessment of our present. The perception exists that 1994 marked the beginning of a rapid escalation in levels of criminal violence.[41] As we'll show, this is not corroborated by the data. South Africa does have high levels of crime, but these certainly did not begin climbing there since 1994. Stressing the long view is not done in an attempt to deflect responsibility or seek forbearance for the painful present. It is an essential route to identifying correctly the nature of the problem. We have collected the official police murder figures going back more than a century and made them as useful and comparable as possible. This allows not just for insight into the likely shape of the real crime victimisation trends, but also gives some hints as to their likely causes and implications. The trend in murder since 1994 has been dramatic and unequivocal. Shockingly, it has received almost no attention or analysis.

Although in precisely the opposite way to what many believe, the last two decades of violence have probably been entirely extraordinary in our history. To help make sense of that pattern, we can look to the relationships between the officially recorded and self-reported victimisation rates of a handful of other crimes. They show that not only has the volume of violence changed dramatically in the last twenty years, but so has its character. Finally, we reflect on what makes crime levels go down, what we can expect to see in the crime rates in the coming years and how we might want to think about shaping that trajectory.

One final note to make before we dive into the numbers: there are going to be quite a lot of them. There are also a lot of references. Don't panic. These are provided so that you can check up on whether what we're saying is reasonable and so that you can easily find where to go for more context and material on these issues. It isn't necessary to take particular note of exactly what the numbers are in order to understand the important arguments in this book. On the other hand, if the numbers are what you're after, the Appendix contains all the official national murder figures and rates since 1911 and the rates of most other major crime types since 1994.

1

—

What are crime statistics?

Every year around September, the South African Police Service (SAPS) produces a number of spreadsheets indicating the number of recorded incidents for each of about 25 major crime types in the preceding year, which runs from 1 April to 31 March. It does so for each station, and provides totals for each province and for the country as a whole. It indicates the change in percentage terms from the previous year and some other reference years, and before 2015 also gave the provincial and national totals as rates per 100 000 people in the appropriate population. Soon after, it also releases an annual report that reflects these figures as graphs, and puts them in the context of annual targets, operational categories, crime reduction strategies and some further information about some of the crimes, for example the size of the businesses targeted in most non-residential robberies or the weapons most commonly used in murders.

This information gets a lot of attention from various quarters and is treated with varying degrees of scepticism. News broadcasts list the highlights and show file footage of police vans flashing their lights, radio hosts opine and ask laypeople to call in with their reactions, experts are asked for comment, infographics are shared, letters are written to the papers, and the police are almost invariably criticised for failing to do enough to control crime. Throughout, it is also often noted that these figures may not be 'reliable' or 'valid'. The reasons for this are seldom clearly spelled out, but often seem largely to reflect a deep mistrust of the police at every level, from the sergeant at the desk all the way up to the National Commissioner and Minister of Police, and sometimes of the value of any quantitative research and of the experts' location in the ivory tower. For reasons of history and politics, it may be that South Africa is a nation unusually wary of the claims made by those in power. Whatever its cause, this scepticism is an excellent starting point for examining any factual claims about our collective social reality, especially given how influential these claims can be. Most conversations about the crime statistics, from the most casual on social media to the most careful in an academic context, will at some stage have to engage with the question of what can reasonably be inferred from them.

A key difficulty with trying to create and make sense of knowledge about crime is that it is by its nature an illicit activity, a thing that someone usually wishes to keep hidden in its entirety or in its details (i.e. who did it). Another problem is that 'crime' is a very broad category of behaviours, including everything from premeditated murder through cable theft and shoplifting, to the consensual buying and selling of items or services that have been deemed inappropriate for legal trade. A third problem is that, especially for the more serious crime types, the participants are people who are considered particularly dangerous and untrustworthy, so can't very easily just be asked to report on their own behaviour.[1] As a result, research on crime will always present more challenges than research into, say, purchasing habits, or anything else that happens relatively openly, is relatively homogeneous and is done by people considered relatively respectable and reliable.

There is also a nearly endless range of things that we may want to know about crime. Its prevalence (how much crime there is in a given place at a given time) may seem like a fairly easy one to get a handle on, but unfortunately this turns out not to be the case. Although we have a number of sources to draw on for this knowledge, of varying degrees of formality and generalisability, each is crucially limited.

Sources of knowledge about crime prevalence

In trying to answer questions about crime, we all have at least four types of sources on which to draw: our own direct experiences; the experiences of others as they filter through to us by word of mouth, the media, local newsletters, and so on;

knowledge based on purposeful research, such as surveys or interviews; and official information.[2] Each of these has its advantages and may be adequate for answering some of the questions we may have about crime, but each is partial, and suffers from different limitations when it comes to the question of how much crime there is.

Knowledge based on our direct personal experiences of crime provides us with extremely rich, contextualised data. Because we gather it ourselves, we can be reasonably sure that it has not been distorted by others' interests. The personal perspective based on being a victim of, witness to or perpetrator of crime is an unrivalled source of detail and emotion in building up the picture of crime. On the other hand, there is no reason to believe that one individual's experience says much about the experiences of the over 50 million other people in the country, so it doesn't help very much with the question of crime prevalence. Of the many things one might reasonably learn from experiencing a house robbery, the frequency of house robberies in general is not one of them. Our own memories, especially when they are traumatic, are a common and tempting but very poor basis for generalisation.

Next there is knowledge that filters through to us from others' direct experiences. Again, this knowledge may be rich in detail and context – we may get a relatively full story in the victim, witness or perpetrator's own words, or as described by someone else, such as a shared neighbour or a journalist. Because the pool from which we are drawing is slightly larger, this knowledge is probably slightly more generalisable than our own experience alone. If we hear about ten house robberies in our suburb this year and only heard about three last year, we may make a tentative claim about the relative frequencies of house robbery in this year and last. However, again we are working with an incomplete picture even of just our area, never mind our city or the country as a whole. We may be missing many people's experiences for a range of reasons, or only hearing about the experiences that make for good stories, or they may have been intentionally or unintentionally distorted in the telling, or we may well just not be as good at remembering things about last year as we think we are. The process of filtering through others can either chaotically or systematically bring an unrepresentative proportion of the incidents to our attention, making this source of information limited in helping to draw good conclusions about how much crime there is.

A third source of knowledge about the prevalence of crime is one more often used by specialists than others with a less academic interest in crime, as it can be expensive to produce and sometimes difficult to interpret. There are many thousands of highly skilled people worldwide whose daily job it is to do quality research on crime, including (but certainly not limited to) on how much of it there is, or whether that is a question that can even be meaningfully answered.[3] They go about this in many different ways, but two of the most common methods of getting a sense of how much crime there is (plus usually a range of related matters) are studies in which people are asked about their experiences of witnessing or being affected by crime, known as victimisation surveys, and ones in which people are asked about their experiences on the other side of the law – known as delinquency surveys. Perhaps the first formal crime survey ever was initiated in 811 by Emperor Charlemagne, and sent to magistrates and nobles to try to get a sense of the reasons for an apparent increase in property crimes in the empire.[4]

Attempts to measure crime and compare populations on the basis of standardised victimisation surveys have the advantage that they can work around some of the flaws and differences in criminal justice system reach and statistical capacity. They can be carefully planned so as to be as systematic and unbiased as possible. The people to be surveyed can be selected in different ways, including so as to make for maximum generalisability. Overall, a key advantage of a survey is that each person can (at least in theory) be asked the same questions in the same ways, which should make it possible to add together and compare their answers. If a suitable selection of people in one place and time reports having experienced house robbery with a certain frequency, and a suitable selection in another place and time report having experienced it at a different frequency, that is a fairly solid basis on which to draw conclusions about those relative frequencies.

There are a number of constraints even on this kind of research. First, when it comes to questions about large populations, conclusions will have to be drawn from the answers of a sample of people rather than every single one. Only the national census attempts to reach every household in the country with its survey questions, and conducting a census involves such huge expense and human and technical capacity, and requires so much planning, that they can't be managed more than every ten years. The vast majority of research instead takes a sample of the population and extrapolates from this to the rest; if done correctly, this is a very reliable method.

More significant limitations to crime surveys include the fact that some victims (or perpetrators) may not be willing to disclose everything in those circumstances (for example, because they fear being blamed, judged or not believed – by the person asking the question or by others in the room); some crimes do not have a clear self-identified victim (for example, the payment of a bribe or the purchase of illegal drugs); some crimes may be too well-hidden for the victims even to know that they have been wronged (for example, corporate fraud); people may not have very good recall (perhaps forgetting some incidents or overestimating the number of times they've happened); and the legal definition of a crime may not correspond with the subjective judgement of it.

What the results of victimisation surveys represent is the crime situation as perceived, memorised and retold under specific conditions by a sample of the population. These surveys have no extraordinary claim to objectivity or accuracy, especially in terms of what is or isn't legal.[5] People have different experiences of and reactions to even those crimes that may share the same careful survey description.[6] A robbery or a sexual assault in South Africa may for many reasons be quite unlike a robbery or sexual assault in Sweden, and this may show up in survey responses in ways that are hard to capture.

Members of communities with high crime levels may be among the least likely to identify lesser infringements as criminal, to remember them and to report them in a survey.[7] For example, when the threat of violent robbery is a daily reality, people may not be in a position to give an accurate account of every minor theft. Another problem with victimisation surveys is that they require large sample sizes in order to be statistically useful, especially for rare crimes.[8] People also have a tendency to 'telescope', that is, to say (without any intention to deceive) that they have been a victim of a crime in the last year, when in fact it happened further back in time.[9] This can result in some crimes being considerably overrepresented in victimisation surveys. Reluctance to discuss sensitive issues with a stranger or in the household context may mean that others are considerably underrepresented. And although the survey designers and field staff may go to every length to align their questions with the same legal definitions and shifting reporting categories used by the police, the respondents may hold very different ideas about what, for example, constitutes assault. Murder, arguably one of the most 'objective' crimes, does not feature on most victimisation surveys, both for reasons of its rarity and for the simple fact that its direct victims aren't known for their loquacity. The results of such surveys can differ by large margins from official police figures even once underreporting is taken into account, so that they are understood in some cases to represent gross overestimations of levels of crime.[10]

Although their 'patina of science'[11] and potentially more independent source makes them especially attractive in places where the authorities are considered untrustworthy, victimisation surveys are not necessarily any better than official murder figures at giving an accurate account of the exact level of crime or violence in a particular place and time. They remain invaluable for what they can reveal about unreported crimes, decisions about reporting and perceptions of crime and justice. And although they are seldom used today to generate estimates of crime *level*, they are still widely used for an understanding of crime *changes*.[12] In other words, they can't tell us how much crime there is, but they can help to determine and corroborate trends over time.

Finally, there is the knowledge about crime that we gain from official sources, which includes figures on the number of alleged or suspected crimes reported to the police, on the number of arrests made, the quantities involved (say, of drugs seized), on the number and proportion of convictions secured, and the number of people sentenced to fine or imprisonment. The practice of systematically collecting and analysing national information on the number of crimes known to the police dates from about the 1830s in France, 1870s in England and Wales, 1930s in the United States, and progressively from about 1913 in South Africa.[13] As noted in the previous chapter, this process has from the first been policy-oriented, and generally driven by officials or people connected to official work.[14] Public officials may be guided by interests quite distinct from, or even opposed to, the pursuit and dissemination of the truth, so concerns about manipulation have been raised from almost the very first.[15]

Even were every relevant official scrupulously honest, however, the information thus produced usually remains the by-product of attempts to govern crime – not so much conducted as pieced together from the paper trail around police work. The case docket, which is where the official trail usually begins, is intended as a practical tool for investigation and potential prosecution, and is not necessarily optimised for statistical research.[16] Only really in the first half of the twentieth century was there a shift in thinking about official crime figures from primarily as useful tools for administrative and law enforcement purposes towards trying to understand and improve their 'accuracy' as a measurement of crime.[17] Because the trouble is, as noted from the start by Adolphe Quetelet, the Belgian statistician who pioneered the use of those early French crime figures, 'our observations can only refer to a certain number of known and tried offences, out of the unknown sum total of crimes committed'.[18]

The clear advantages of official statistics are that they have the potential to be consistent and systematic, and to reflect the behaviour and experiences not of a sample of the total population, but of every case that has successfully run the gauntlet between a possibly criminal action and its police acknowledgement. Their greatest disadvantage is that this process of winnowing can be gruelling.[19] As with victimisation surveys, an event must pass the tests of being detected by someone, identified as possibly criminal, considered appropriate and worthwhile to bring to a stranger's attention, and remembered and recounted substantially accurately.

In addition, to make it into the official statistics, someone must deem the event appropriate to warrant not just mention but the opening of a formal docket, it must be recognised as criminal and correctly categorised by the police officer on duty, substantially accurately recorded, sometimes verified by police work (to determine, for example, that a car reported stolen is not still in the garage and part of an insurance scam), the data properly captured and preserved, the large volume of separate incidents collated, and finally the results publicised in a useful format. An unknown proportion of incidents that we may be interested in and consider to be criminal never make it through this process. This is known as the dark, or hidden, figure of crime, and it haunts all attempts to measure it, make sense of it, and build theory around it.

The hidden figure and what to make of it

The size and shape of the hidden figure, often envisioned as the submerged portion of an iceberg, varies by crime type, by victim type, by a range of surrounding social factors and by just as many factors within the criminal justice system. Changes in the recorded crime rate may represent just a change in the waterline of the iceberg of crime, rather than a change in its size or shape. Victimisation surveys are a key source of information on the hidden figure, as respondents are usually asked whether or not they reported all the crimes they have experienced, and their reasons for that decision. Chief among these reasons are usually assessments of the seriousness of the crime, how difficult the reporting process is expected to be and how the police are likely to react, and whether there is some other benefit, such as for insurance purposes. Research that examines instead the processes at play within law enforcement institutions can also shed light on why and how some things slip between the cracks. Reasons may include intentional tampering so as to meet crime reduction targets (for example, downgrading reports from crimes considered more serious, such as attempted housebreaking, to less serious ones, such as malicious damage to property), capacity constraints (say, because dockets are not properly tracked and electronically captured) and features of institutional culture (officers may not be inclined to open dockets for sexual crimes or crimes against foreigners). In some cases, discrepancies may arise from administrative norms, such as whether every crime or just the most serious in an incident is recorded, or whether the fact of there being multiple victims or perpetrators involved in one incident results in the opening of multiple dockets.[20]

Whenever official crime statistics are discussed, the subject should be qualified – ideally, explicitly – as *recorded* crime statistics, or crime statistics *as known to and acknowledged by the police.* For some crimes, this qualification may be so significant that the statistics have very limited usefulness. Other forms of research suggest that although the exact extent of underreporting is unclear, it is particularly large for sexual crimes.[21] This means that estimates of total prevalence and apparent trends based on official sexual crime statistics should be interpreted with extreme caution, as they are perhaps the least likely of all the crimes to represent an accurate reflection of reality. At the other end of the spectrum is murder, which is readily measurable, clearly and quite consistently defined, and relatively well-reported or discovered. True, some violent deaths may not ever be reported, some dead bodies may not ever be found, some may be incorrectly ascribed to accident, suicide or natural causes, and there may be administrative complications such as failures to revise attempted murder dockets to murder when victims succumb to injuries or the listing of multiple murders from a single incident in one docket. These are problems everywhere in the world. As a general rule, however, murder figures are considered the gold standard of crime statistics. Whereas variation in reporting dynamics may skew results for other crime types considerably – making it difficult to determine whether an observed difference in crime statistics across jurisdictions or across time is the result of a real difference in crime or rather a difference in social, political or institutional factors – variation in murder figures is generally considered to be robust. A large and relatively stable proportion of the iceberg of murder is visible above the waterline of official recording.

When recorded official figures for sexual crimes such as rape show a downward trend, it may be that there has indeed been a decrease in those crimes, but it may equally be (and is often interpreted to mean) that fewer incidents are passing through the process between the event and its acknowledgement in police figures. It may, for example, reflect a decline in popular faith in the criminal justice system's being of any assistance. When recorded official figures for murder show a significant downward trend, it is probably safe to conclude that murder has indeed declined. For the range of crimes with underreporting incentives and rates somewhere in the middle, it can be difficult to make sense of the trends. Are recorded official burglary rates declining because there are fewer burglaries happening, because people are increasingly unconvinced that the police will be able to do anything useful about the burglaries they may report, because the police are wherever possible avoiding opening burglary dockets, or some combination of these and other factors? The statistics alone can't answer this question, so it is here that other forms of research, especially victimisation surveys, are particularly important.

Given all these difficulties, it can be tempting to write the official statistics off as too hopelessly compromised to be of much use in working out how much of what kind of crime there is. Many people do so, having come to that conclusion based on different considerations and from different ideological and/or theoretical starting points. Given, however, that all our other potential sources of such knowledge are also tremendously imperfect, such an approach strikes us as unwarranted and reckless. To the extent that such a socially complex phenomenon as crime is measurable at all, the official statistics remain one of the best tools available. When combined, wherever possible, with knowledge from other sources, and when handled with sufficient understanding of their limitations and likely distortions, official statistics can help reveal things about the prevalence of crime that would otherwise be unknown.

Moreover, their basis in official state processes and their relative simplicity mean that a principled reluctance to engage with the crime statistics is unlikely ever to be shared by a critical mass within policy circles or popular opinion. The crime statistics will continue to be important whether or not they are of good quality or well understood. As such, it is difficult to justify leaving their assessment, interpretation and development to those less exacting in evidentiary requirements, less attentive to bureaucratic pressures and flaws, and less critical of the circus of overinterpretation and underfinesse that spirals wildly, albeit briefly, around the annual release of the statistics. In short, the crime statistics are a blunt and potentially misleading tool but not more so than the others on hand, they aren't going away, and there is likely more to be lost by ignoring them than by engaging with them.

Crime statistics and police performance

The reasons why crime rates differ between places and change across time are hotly contested. Many countries have seen a number of major swings in their crime rates within their recorded history, and for each of those shifts there are usually at least a handful of major competing explanations. For example, crime rates in a number of countries (including the United Kingdom and United States) saw an unanticipated fall in the 1990s, and according to one list there have been 21 different hypotheses proposed – from fairly standard ones about policing, economics and demographics to unorthodox and inevitably more titillating ones around abortion access and lead poisoning.[22] Statistically and theoretically untangling the complexity of our societies in order to reach conclusions about causes is an endless challenge for social researchers. It may surprise many people to know that there isn't, in fact, any consensus among experts about whether at least the short- to medium-term actions of the criminal justice system have much to do with falling crime rates.

When it comes to big, sustained swings in crime, it seems that the key factors do include some broad measure of the rule of law, but equally include the wider patterns of our social and political lives, especially whether the state and society are stable, functional and accountable to one other.[23] The actions of the police play a part in this, but they are by no means in a position to shape it on their own. On the one hand, there are things that the police can do to prevent at least some crimes (notably by focusing their attention very narrowly on the places where crime is highest,[24] and by using a problem-oriented approach that draws many tools and actors together rather than a one-size-fits-all one based on standard policing procedures).[25] There are also things they can do to foster a shared sense of normative purpose with citizens and to encourage compliance with the law.[26] But, on the other hand, crime rates often fluctuate with no relationship to changes in policing methods.[27]

The exception to this is the handful of crimes that, although they may directly and indirectly go on to do considerable harm, do not necessarily at the moment of their commission have a clear, self-identified victim. Or the 'victim' may be the same person as the 'perpetrator'. Therefore, rather than relying primarily on people bringing these crimes to their attention, the police must usually go out and find them. These are called 'police-detected crimes', or crimes heavily dependent on police action for detection. In South Africa such crimes are illegal possession of firearms or ammunition, drug-related crime, driving under the influence of alcohol or other drugs and, more recently, sexual crimes detected as a result of police action (largely sex-work-related crimes). What is counterintuitive about this kind of crime is that when police are highly active and effective at targeting these crimes, their rates should (at least in the short term) go up, regardless of how many of them are actually happening. This makes it difficult to determine whether rising rates of police-detected crimes are a sign of more of these things happening, or because the police are, for example, staging many more roadblocks and raids. The rates within an area often go up one year and down the next in accordance with fluctuations in policing priorities. Whereas police stations' performance measurement mechanisms incentivise officers to reduce the official rates of other crimes, for these crimes there are formal or informal quotas, and their numbers are seen in a positive light.[28] Target chasing for these crimes may spur the police to do good work, but it may equally spur them to do busy work, for example by arresting numerous drug users in an area to make a quota but leaving untouched the drug dealers whose removal would make it more difficult to meet quotas in future. Further, because the people involved with these crimes have little reason to report themselves even to those other than the police, non-specialised victimisation surveys haven't bothered with asking about them. To an even greater extent than with other crimes, when these rates change, we don't in fact have much idea whether it's a good thing or a bad thing.

Most crimes are not police-detected, but are reported to the police by the public – usually by the victims. Although the police are not powerless about how many of these there are, to a large extent the crime rate is not within their control, especially in terms of its long-term ballpark figure. This is the case even in places without the constraints faced by a developing country with tightly limited resources and very high crime rates. Yet the SAPS is tasked under the National Development Plan with creating a South Africa in which everyone is and feels safe, and police members at every level, from the individual officer through the station commander all the way up to the National Commissioner are held responsible for the crime figures recorded on their watch.[29] This would be like basing the praise, punishment and promotion of medical doctors (who also have some but limited power over the health of their patients) on how many of certain diagnoses they make. An officer's preliminary diagnosis of crime, with a view to further investigation and possible eventual confirmation by a court, is precisely what our crime statistics are based on. Setting targets for something that (if even possible) is far harder to achieve than to fake is a recipe for deception.

Little surprise, then, that accusations of 'cooking the statistics' are commonplace. Anecdotal evidence abounds that the police are sometimes reluctant or entirely unwilling to open dockets, that dockets of cases deemed unsolvable are quietly destroyed rather than entered on to the central administration system, and that offences are 'downgraded' to the least serious crime into which they can possibly be twisted.[30] This is by no means the case only in South Africa, as exemplified in a recent spat between successive police commissioners in New York about whether crime statistics were being manipulated, for example by failing to record people with graze wounds as shooting victims, or by labelling as self-inflicted the wounds of uncooperative victims.[31]

Even without deliberate attempts to finesse the data, it has long been known that the police exercise considerable discretion over whether and how to respond officially to reported or detected incidents of rule-breaking,[32] especially for crimes considered at all debatable. Research suggests that attempts to report sexual assault or rape to the police are often dismissed entirely as presumed fictions, as representing normal or justifiable sexual behaviour, or as having no prospect of successful prosecution (because it'll just be 'he said, she said').[33] Where discretion can't extend to the fact of official recording, it may extend to its content. Despite consistent official guidelines, what one officer initially records as attempted murder another might record as assault with the intent to inflict grievous bodily harm (assault GBH). The markedly more unstable historical pattern shown in rates of attempted murder compared to those of murder suggest that recording practices (or institutionalised discretion) for attempted murder have seen considerable fluctuation. The extent to which discretion and manipulation distort the crime statistics is unclear, but other research, such as victims of crime surveys and studies on police institutional practices and cultures, might shed some light.

Perhaps in order to get itself out of the bind of both needing to justify its funding and powers and needing to avoid being blamed for trends beyond its control, the SAPS for a few years argued that crimes can be distinguished on the basis of their 'policeability', or the extent to which they can be prevented by police action.[34] This was based on the reasoning that the conditions in which some crimes occur are such that they allow for more or less of the spectrum of conventional policing methodology, such as patrols, public warnings or crime mapping.[35]

Such an attempt to introduce nuance into efforts to hold police responsible for the crime rate is commendable. Unfortunately the policeability distinction (which the SAPS no longer seems to make use of in public planning or reporting) was inconsistently applied and was rather a unilateral declaration than the result of any apparent empirical evidence or consultation.[36] The concept of variation in policeability – that some crimes can probably more feasibly be prevented by police than others – is a useful one, but there is simply no broadly accepted basis on which to make the distinction.

In short, the extent to which the number of crimes recorded by the police is a measure of police performance is limited at best. The police are by no means powerless, but to a large extent both the ballpark figure and the smaller fluctuations in crime levels are beyond their direct control. To hold them responsible solely or even primarily for the number of crimes they record is a recipe for frustration and deception. The prevention of crime may be an appropriate police mandate, but the reduction of the number of crimes they record is not.

A large part of police work is purely administrative. They are a 24-hour-a-day representative of the state, imbued with the almost magical power to 'certify' documents, events and people into officialdom. Often, this is all that people expect of them. The insurance company requires that you provide a case number to account for a loss or the potential employer requires proof of your lack of a criminal record. Sometimes, what people want from the police is immediate protection and recognition, with no need to do much following up. Many charges laid on chaotic Friday and Saturday nights are withdrawn come Monday. But another important part of what police do is kick into motion the machinery of the criminal justice system. What the police and rest of the criminal justice system have far more control over than the recorded number of crimes, and what we should be keeping a far closer eye on, is what happens *after* a crime is reported. These are the crime statistics by which we should make sense of police performance.

The other crime statistics

We know that much of the crime that people in South Africa experience never gets reported to the police, mostly because victims don't think the police can or will do anything about it anyway.[37] When people do report a crime to the police, if they're satisfied with the interaction, it's usually because the police came to the scene of the crime; if they're dissatisfied, it's usually because the police took too long to respond.[38] Of course most people would prefer it if the crime never happened in the first place, but given that it did and that they reported it to (or it was uncovered by) the police, what matters to victims of crime is what happens next.

At a station level, police performance is tracked in accordance with a standardised chart, which includes measures of progress towards a range of targets in crime prevention, crime reaction, crime investigation, human resource management, physical resource (e.g. vehicle) management and data integrity.[39] Although weighted heavily to crime prevention (i.e. reducing the number of crimes recorded) this system also generates other numerical measures of police performance at the station level that can be aggregated to the province and country. The chart's focus on quantitative targets that encourage manipulation or number-chasing, its failure to measure customer satisfaction or public confidence, and its one-size-fits-all attempt at evaluating and comparing stations facing vastly different crime and other conditions are serious problems, and they are problems grappled with by police agencies the world over.[40] Much of the other performance data from the chart and other sources already appears in the SAPS annual reports, but it gets nowhere near as much public attention as the recorded crime figures.[41] Although there may be a risk that routinely bringing this kind of data more prominently into the public eye will further raise incentives to manipulate it directly or through empty target-chasing, it would represent a major improvement on publicly assessing the police on just the one item. There is no single international model for how to monitor police performance, but there has for some years been a trend towards the use of a range of indicators of policing outputs and impact.[42]

The SAPS annual report indicates progress towards dozens of performance indicators within its various sub-programmes. A few we should be keeping better track of include the number of stolen/robbed vehicles recovered in relation to the number of vehicles reported as stolen/robbed (53 per cent in 2014/2015,

67 per cent in 2013/2014); the number of escapees from police custody (697 in 2014/2015, 1 017 in 2013/2014); and the average national reaction time to calls categorised as serious complaints in progress (18:26 minutes in 2014/2015, 19:02 minutes in 2013/2014, 18:46 in 2012/2013).[43] To track these indicators is not necessarily to seek simply to improve the numbers. More roadblocks or more arrests do not necessarily make for better policing. But they do give us a much better idea of what the police are doing with their time than the recorded crime figures. The performance indicators that should arguably matter most for our assessments of whether or not justice is being done are those that track what happens to case dockets after they are opened.

If every crime alleged at the police charge desk resulted in a conviction, we wouldn't need a criminal justice system at all, and could save a great deal of time and money by simply letting people dispense punishment privately as and when they felt it justified and could get their hands on a possible culprit. Instead, most organised societies have (at least officially) opted for a situation where those with criminal grievances contact the police and thereby knock at the door of a large, inevitably imperfect and often underresourced system that is tasked with making a host of difficult decisions. Many more cases enter into the criminal justice system than make it through to the other end. It works like a series of sieves, winnowing the numbers down at every stage.[44] The extent of the sieve effect varies between countries and between crimes, and each step varies in the extent to which it is systematic or random, hidden or documented, and justified or unjust in the kind of society in which we want to live. There are trade-offs involved. Maximising the proportion of charges that result in criminal punishment may involve sacrifices in rights, and the criminalisation of people and actions that don't warrant it. Minimising that proportion may undermine the system's credibility to the point where victims and communities resort to extralegal solutions. So whereas the number of crimes recorded tells us something about the kind of society we are, the numbers that unfold after that tell us about the kind of society we want to be and are creating. The latter numbers are also considerably more revealing about the effectiveness of the relevant institutions.

When a crime is reported and a case docket opened, the key thing that should happen next is that it is followed up. Each case should be investigated: details and cooperation should be sought from victims and witnesses; physical evidence should be secured, documented and processed; if possible, the alleged perpetrator should be identified, located and arrested; and if appropriate the case should be prepared and referred for trial to the separate institution of the prosecutor. The prosecutor must then decide whether the case is worth pursuing and, if so, how to go about doing so. The case against the accused should then be thoroughly contested in court so that a judge or magistrate can decide whether it has been sufficiently proven and, if so, what the appropriate response is on the part of the state.

Depending on how this process unfolds, each incident of

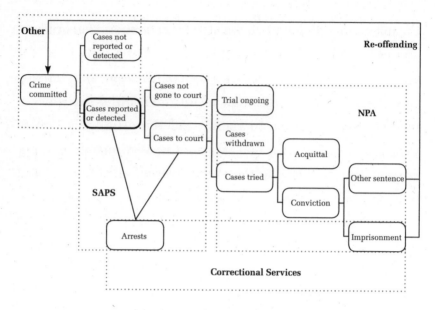

Figure 1: The official paths of crime, showing the range of things that generate 'crime statistics' and indicating broad institutional responsibility for documentation

possible or alleged crime will eventually settle officially somewhere along a path that looks something like that shown in Figure 1.

The contents of the box outlined in bold in Figure 1 represent the sum of what most people think of as 'the crime statistics', but there are (or should be) numerical data available for every other point on this route. They are all crime statistics. Each makes a lot more sense within the context of the others than it does on its own.

Most reported cases don't ever make it to court. Those that do may then go on to be withdrawn in court (usually because of insufficient evidence), may have their trial delayed and ongoing for a long time, may be finalised otherwise (for example, through alternative dispute resolution for minors or less serious crimes), may finish their trial but be awaiting a verdict, and may eventually be finalised with a verdict. That verdict may be either an acquittal (not guilty) or a conviction (guilty). Conviction is followed by sentencing, which may or may not take the form of imprisonment. It isn't clear exactly how the relationships between these outcomes should inform our assessment of whether the police, the prosecuting authority or the courts have been successful. For example, whose success or failure is it when a victim withdraws a charge or when a prosecutor decides not to take a case?[45]

As much as the public is understandably interested in how many of which alleged crimes were recorded by the police, it should and probably would be equally interested in how those crimes end up being resolved by the criminal justice system. Unfortunately, figuring this out turns out to be difficult. The problem is that the various sources and formats of figures don't connect with each other in a useful way. There have over almost the last two decades been huge investments in establishing and implementing an integrated criminal justice electronic information system. This is designed to link data, where possible, between the SAPS, the Department of Justice and Constitutional Development, Legal Aid South Africa, the National Prosecuting Authority (NPA), and the Department of Correctional Services. Progress has been slow, and it isn't yet possible to track individual cases through the system on an ongoing basis.

Most attempts to quantify what is happening therefore have to rely on the recorded incidence of various events in the same time period. So, for example, for one year we can find out from the police how many alleged cases were recorded and how many arrests were made, from the NPA how many convictions there were, and from Correctional Services how the prison population size changed – but these are not necessarily the same cases. In fact, very few cases are resolved in the same year and under exactly the same charges as which they are reported.[46]

Large-scale studies that track a sample of individual cases through the system to work out how they fare are expensive, time-consuming and rare. As crime patterns and institutions change, their results may quickly become out of date. One study took a sample of crimes reported between January 1997 and April 1998, and checked to see where the cases had got to about two years later. It found that for murder, for example, 61 per cent of the cases reported had not yet gone to court, 8 per cent had been withdrawn, 12 per cent still had trials ongoing, 8 per cent resulted in a verdict of not-guilty, and 11 per cent in a verdict of guilty.[47] The conviction rates so measured – as a proportion of the number of cases reported rather than the number of verdicts given – compared quite badly internationally for murder and rape, but in fact quite well for robbery.[48] There hasn't been a similar study since. Instead, we are forced to rely on the yearly review method, which can only give a very rough view of what is happening at different points in the criminal justice process.

The SAPS tracks its crime-solving performance according to the detection rate, the trial-ready docket rate and the conviction rate. To varying degrees, these are determined by the nature of the charges and the decisions made by, and quality of the work of, the police, the prosecutor and the judge or magistrate. The detection rate is calculated as 'the total number of charges referred to court added to charges withdrawn before court, plus charges closed as unfounded divided by the total number of charges reported and brought forward and expressed as a percentage'.[49] More simply, this represents the proportion of charges where sufficient evidence was gathered to go to trial if appropriate. Crucially, it involves identifying and charging a suspect. Once that has happened, the docket must be fully investigated and finalised for trial. The trial-ready docket rate is determined when 'the total number of case dockets certified as "investigation finalised" on the [SAPS's] CAS [Crime Administration System] are divided by the total number of outstanding charges and is expressed as a percentage'.[50] It represents the proportion of cases that don't require any further investigation by the police. The conviction rate is determined by 'the number of charges resulting in a guilty verdict divided by the sum of the guilty and not guilty verdicts and is expressed as a percentage'.[51] It represents the outcomes of that small proportion of charges that did make it all the way through to end in a verdict, and it is only at this point that we should really stop referring to the charges as 'alleged'. These various numbers represent snapshots of the process through which a case might travel, but they don't connect with each other in such a way that we can properly track what is happening.

We can note simply, for example, that there were about a quarter as many convictions for murder in 2014/2015 as there were murder cases recorded.[52] In other words, for every 100 murders recorded in 2014/2015, there were 24 convictions. For all contact crimes combined, the detection rate is higher, at about 54 per cent, but the effective yearly conviction rate is only about 9 per cent.[53] For all property-related crimes, it's about 15 per cent detected and an effective 4 per cent convicted.[54] This isn't quite as dismal as it sounds. In comparison, the UK's effective conviction rate for violent crimes against the person is about 15 per cent, and for theft offences is about 11 per cent[55] – and this with far lower crime rates and far greater resources with which to respond to crime.

There are even more publicly available numbers about crime that we should track and that can tell us more important things about the criminal justice process than the sum of crimes it recorded at its front end. Examples include the relative numbers of police personnel and private security officers, the number of people currently imprisoned without having been found guilty, the extent of prison overcrowding, where police are allocated and how they spend their time, how many suspects they kill in the course of their duties, and how many of them kill themselves. If we want to know how the police and the rest of the criminal justice system are doing at creating the kind of society in which we want to live, these other statistics around crime are where we should be focusing a lot more of our attention. Still, as long as we have a good sense of the constraints to interpreting the recorded counts of alleged or suspected crimes, they can serve as a valuable barometer of how the people, places and activities in our world, country, cities and homes have come to be organised. Before we get stuck into that, we still need to consider why this is even more difficult in the South African context than in many of the places to which we might wish to compare it.

2

The South African crime statistics context

Many of the problems with interpreting official crime figures are fairly universal; they are shared by every administrative area that seeks to collect such data. Researchers in Switzerland and Swaziland alike must grapple with the significance of the range of possible factors that compromise the usefulness of their crime statistics for determining the prevalence of crime and functioning of the criminal justice system. And, especially in the last three decades, an increasing scrutiny and criticism of the accuracy and value of crime statistics has proliferated all over the world.[1]

There are also, however, some factors that make the South African crime statistics particularly tricky. Chief among these is our fraught history of policing and governance, which not only undermines any attempt to get decent data about crime prior to 1994, but also has had lingering effects on the quality of our statistics since. Although older piecemeal crime and justice figures did exist, crime statistics on anywhere near national level began to be maintained only from about 1913, following the formation of the Union of South Africa and the amalgamation of various colonial police forces into the new South African Police (SAP).[2] The first half of the twentieth century already featured policing that was starkly racist, with black South Africans for the most part enduring not protection but either brutality or neglect.[3] Under apartheid, the SAP was less an agency of crime recording, prevention and response than it was a counterinsurgency force targeted at political enemies, itself often responsible for the commission and promotion of serious crimes.[4] It has been said that by the 1980s between 30 per cent and 40 per cent of SAP staff were dedicated just to 'stabilising' political 'unrest',[5] and that only about 10 per cent were focused on crime detection and investigation.[6] The enforcement of influx control and the range of other race-related laws, the protection of the border and the difficulty in recruiting and retaining both black and white employees made for chronic understaffing.[7] Thousands of *kitskonstabels* (instant constables) and municipal police were appointed to put uniforms on the streets, but they received meagre training and often lacked basic literacy or skills.[8]

The limited resources that were concerned with crime fighting were disproportionately allocated to white suburbs and business districts, which in 1994 hosted three-quarters of the country's police stations.[9] By contrast, based on anecdotal data, for a century or more most of the country's violent crime incidents took place in black urban and peri-urban settlements.[10] Here, the police were extremely thin on the ground when it came to non-political crime-related work, and although community–police relations were in some cases rather more nuanced than outright antagonism, in others the police were akin to an occupying army, receiving little or no legitimacy from those they sought to control.[11] Instead, these areas often relied on the justice dispensed by street committees and 'community courts',[12] which had complex relationships with more formal policing and with political and criminal interests.[13] Policing in the so-called Bantustans or 'independent homelands' was also deeply compromised; although the local police forces were ostensibly beyond SAP jurisdiction, they were trained and to varying degrees directed by the apartheid state.[14] 'Homeland' police forces were rapidly established and chaotically managed,[15] fared even worse than the SAP in terms of resources, were notoriously brutal – especially in KwaZulu and Bophuthatswana – and had a perhaps even more tenuous grip on public legitimacy.[16] Little or no attempt was made to keep a record of even those crimes that were reported or detected. At the time of amalgamation, in 1995, the combined 'homeland' forces, which had served about 40 per cent of the national population, made up about 20 per cent of the new South African Police Service.[17]

Prior to 1994, most South Africans likely saw very little use in reporting crime to the police, and the police in turn placed a very low priority on detecting, investigating and recording the crimes experienced by the majority of the population. At the same time, data related to law enforcement and defence institutions was closely guarded, with scrutiny or criticism easily characterised as subverting the fragile 'national interest'.[18] As a cumulative result, crime statistics prior to 1994 are of very poor quality. It is overwhelmingly likely that for most crime types, only a small proportion of the incidents made it into any official statistics, which did not meaningfully or at all cover large parts of the country.[19] Estimates of population size and distribution were also poor and highly politically charged, such that it remains unclear how many people lived where, and therefore what we should make of the figures that do exist. This makes it very difficult to make sense of longer-term trends in crime.

Unfortunately, this history also complicates interpretation of any of the trends since 1994, as few of the factors that compromise the older data had any prospect of disappearing overnight. In 1994, the official national crime figure totals abruptly included those recorded against the roughly 16 million people in the Bantustans, but issues of station location, resource allocation, police focus, capacity and culture at all levels, data management and popular legitimacy could not be so quickly remedied. On the one hand, there remain some areas in the country where station capacity and the relationships between the police and the community are such that, despite being very high, the official crime figures probably reflect a fraction of all the crime suffered by residents. On the other hand, a gradual improvement in these factors – as might reasonably be expected under a fundamentally transformed political and security regime and in response to widespread attempts to reform community–police relations – would be indistinguishable in the statistics from a real change in crime, such that especially an increase in recorded crime could be entirely a 'statistical illusion'.[20]

Other relatively rapid social changes during this broad period (common in developing countries) could also drive shifts in reporting dynamics, further distorting the statistical trends. For example, improvements in gender equality and the recognition of gender-based violence may result in growing numbers of such crimes being reported and recorded, while economic growth and the expansion of the insurance industry could mean more people reporting property crimes in order to make claims.[21] Developing countries also tend to have higher levels of especially violent crime than developed countries,[22] but also to have relatively poor statistical reach.[23] So South Africa may be increasingly unfortunate in combining on the one hand its slow improvement in human development,[24] and on the other its relatively high crime reporting rates,[25] and its relatively good and improving statistical capacity.[26] In other words, we are cursed by having a lot to count plus being quite good at counting.

As of amalgamation into the SAPS in 1995, every reported crime in the country was required to be registered on the electronic Crime Administration System (CAS), but proper use of

CAS didn't immediately catch on. Police crime analysts quickly noted that CAS data was unacceptably poor, especially as it was compromised by negative attitudes towards it, with stations struggling to see the cumbersome system's operational usefulness in combating crime. In 1997, the then Minister for Safety and Security, Sydney Mufamadi, therefore appointed a Committee of Inquiry into the Collection, Processing and Publication of Crime Statistics, consisting of a number of local and international experts (including one of the authors, Shaw) under the leadership of Dr Mark Orkin, then Head of Statistics South Africa and later CEO of the Human Sciences Research Council.

The recommendations of the Orkin Committee, presented to the minister in 1998, led to the progressive implementation of a number of measures to improve the validity of the statistics, including the reorganisation and streamlining of the CAS system, the development of training programmes, manuals and guidelines for its use, the provision of hundreds of additional computers to police stations, and the employment and training of thousands of staff at various levels to do the typing and analysis.[27] In the course of this process, the new minister, Steve Tshwete, announced a temporary pause or moratorium on the release of crime statistics in mid-2000, ostensibly in order to ease pressure on the system as it worked to consolidate the numerous changes. There was considerable public outcry, as it was believed that the moratorium was intended to serve political ends, and especially to hide a spiralling crime rate. The moratorium was lifted about a year later, in 2001, although major changes to the crime registration systems continued to be implemented for months afterwards. As a result, it is only as of about 2003 that there has been much prospect of consistent methodology in generating our crime statistics. In other words, there are three broad historical bands of data quality and comparability in the South African crime statistics: everything prior to 1994, for which the data is incomplete and very poor; the period between 1995 and 2002, for which the data is inconsistent and may be progressively improving in quality; and the period from 2003, for which the data is relatively consistent and complete.

Basic procedural consistency and geographic coverage do not, unfortunately, guarantee accuracy. Although a number of the technical and institutional hurdles between a crime incident and its correct appearance in the statistics have been reduced, many others remain. Among these is the problem we've already discussed – that rather than primarily the quality of this data, the people who control it are consistently evaluated on its content. Because the police have such a strong interest in making their crime data look a certain way, we should compare its accuracy with other sources wherever possible.

The quality of the SAPS murder statistics

Police everywhere in the world have been accused of manipulating their crime figures, of 'cooking the books', for as long as

they have collected and disseminated them. The SAPS is regularly accused of trying to make itself and the crime situation
look better by wherever possible squeezing the numbers into
a better shape. In a lot of research and thinking about crime,
most or even all the analytical weight is placed on the recorded
figures of just one crime type: murder. There are a number of
reasons why murder numbers are less subject than most crimes
to such squeezing.

Although there is no legal requirement that ordinary people report most suspected crimes to the police, South Africa
has a strict death registration system. The Births and Deaths
Registration Act requires that every death in the country and
of a South African abroad be reported to an authorised party,
and if such a party has reasonable doubt about whether the
death was due to natural causes, the police must be informed.
Having been informed of an apparently unnatural death, the
SAPS must record and proceed to investigate it under one of
three categories: murder, which is intentional killing; culpable
homicide, which is killing that is unlawful but unintentional
or negligent (i.e. accidents); or inquest, which applies to deaths
that require some investigation but are believed not to be due
to another person (chiefly suicides).[28] The police decision as to
what kind of docket to open is provisional. The final decision
may only be made in court many years later, and – as the Oscar
Pistorius case has driven into the heads of the world – even
this may not clarify matters satisfactorily. There have been
isolated accusations that police may sometimes opt to record

as culpable homicides or inquests what should really be murders.[29] The police may also intentionally or unintentionally fail to manage the dockets properly and to register them on the centralised system. Luckily, we have a couple of ways in which we can check up on how many murders are slipping between the cracks and failing to make it into the SAPS figures.

The biggest single factor keeping the murder figures honest is, to put it crudely, the corpse. There are certainly circumstances under which dead bodies may not be found, reported to any official authority or correctly identified as murders. The SAPS website currently lists about 200 missing people. It may be that a considerable number of these and the many other unreported missing people have in fact been murdered, but they will be considered missing until more evidence is found or they are legally presumed dead. Repeat killers in particular may be good at disguising their crimes, such that the only way to get information on their numbers is by asking the killers themselves. Interviews with serial killers and contract killers are not unheard of, but they are rare and are constrained by issues especially of self-selection and reliability.[30] Although pinning down definitions is an ongoing problem, it has been said that South Africa has a large number of serial killers for its size.[31] Defined as occurring 'when a suspect(s) murder two or more victims on at least two separate occasions and the motive for the homicides are not primarily for material gain nor to eliminate a witness in another matter', the SAPS has identified 131 homicide series between 1953 and 2007, of which 74 per cent were solved.[32] This represents a tiny proportion of the total known murders in this time. It may well be that a fair number of such murders are never discovered, but at least by something like the above definition, serial murders are generally understood to be rare, comprising less than 1 per cent of murders.[33]

But as long as there is someone who knows about and reports a death, there should somewhere be a record of it. Murder involves not just a criminal act but the end of a legal subject (official personhood) and the new presence of a distinctive object (the dead body), with the result that besides the police there are at least in theory two other relatively official sources on the number of murders: vital registration systems (which try to keep some official record of all the people within a country) and medical facilities. Few low- and middle-income countries have either such forms of data of reasonable quality or at all, and those in South Africa prior to 1994 are considered extremely compromised for many of the same reasons as are those from criminal justice sources.[34] They have become increasingly useful since then.

The quality of mortality data from vital registration systems depends on their coverage and completeness, the precision of their cause-of-death recording and the reliability of that attribution.[35] We've said that South Africa has quite a strict death registration system, which requires reporting of all deaths to the Department of Home Affairs or someone otherwise authorised to receive such reports. The coverage and quality of the National Population Register has improved over the years, and it has most recently been estimated to be about 94 per cent complete (for adult deaths) as compared to census data.[36] Statistics South Africa, which collects all the completed death notification forms from the Department of Home Affairs, and cleans, categorises and analyses the data, has indicated that in 2014 deaths due to non-natural causes, or what are 'external causes of morbidity and mortality', comprised 10.5 per cent or 47 761 of the 453 360 total registered deaths.[37] Of these, about 11 per cent, or 5 314, were ascribed to assault, while the rest included accidents of various kinds (55 per cent), events of 'undetermined intent' (17 per cent), transport accidents (12 per cent) and intentional self-harm (1.2 per cent).[38]

Rather than rely on the official registration documents, it is also possible to go directly to mortuaries (or 'medico-legal laboratories') and get their data from death registers, which include basic information on all deaths, or from postmortem reports, which are required for all non-natural deaths. Mortuary-based approaches have not yet overcome problems of funding, tangled institutional responsibility and the sheer volume of data spread across over a hundred locations countrywide to obtain full and continuous national coverage of the roughly half a million deaths in the country each year, but instead base their national estimates on samples and complicated statistical weightings.[39] These samples are seldom random, and may introduce their own problems for generalisability.[40] Other key problems in data from death registers and the national vital registration system are that their categorisation tends to reflect better the nature of the injury (e.g. head injury) than its underlying cause (e.g. whether due to assault),[41] and that the international convention is to record as accidental those injury deaths with limited information on intent.[42] Although improving, cause-of-death data in South Africa is not yet considered to be of good quality, partly because too large a proportion of deaths are registered as being ill-defined or of undetermined intent.[43] Collecting the results of full postmortem investigations can help give a more accurate view of the causes of injury-related mortality, but again there is no national system that collects these.[44]

Coverage and problems with data linkage between different institutional processes also make it difficult to validate, track, and compare these sources of data. Their results vary by large margins, with mortuary-based estimates usually higher than the SAPS figure, and vital registration results far lower. So for example in 2009, the SAPS announced that it had recorded 18 148 murders in the preceding financial year (April to March). Mortuary data led to an estimate of 19 028 homicides in the 2009 calendar year (January to December).[45] That's a discrepancy of about 5 per cent. Statistics South Africa said there had been 49 456 deaths registered as due to any non-natural causes, of which 5 089 were considered due to assault and 6 683 were due to events of undetermined intent.[46] Despite the discrepancies, which have been higher in the past, the trends in the sources over time have been consistent with each other,[47] and the distribution of murder within the country suggested by the SAPS appears to be largely sound.[48]

But we can do a little better than this. There are some regions and years for which there is full coverage of mortuary figures, and we can compare these quite well to police figures, although usually the dates of coverage do not perfectly align, as other sources tend to use the calendar year whereas the SAPS uses the financial year. The discrepancy in the Western Cape, which is fairly consistently monitored, has tended to be less than 5 per cent, and in some years less than 1 per cent.[49] That in Gauteng appears to be somewhere in the region of 10 per cent,[50] and in Mpumalanga it may be closer to 20 per cent.[51]

A number of factors may contribute to these discrepancies. The SAPS may of course undercount due to deliberate manipulation, for example by miscategorising deaths. Its figure may also lose some numbers to infrastructural, training or procedural constraints,[52] for example when multiple murders are incorrectly listed on one docket or when attempted murder dockets are not changed to murder when victims succumb to injuries.[53] Mpumalanga's relatively large discrepancy may point to difficulties with capacity. There is also the possibility that some proportion of murders may simply never be reported to the police. In 2015, 95 per cent of those who said in a survey that their household had recently lost someone to murder also said that they had reported it to the police.[54] This suggests about 5 per cent of murders may not be brought to police attention by the victims' households, and although health facilities and mortuaries are required to do so, some may fail to.

Unfortunately there is little we can do to quantify the

unnatural deaths that never even make it on to a mortuary register. Surveys can ask people directly about the murders of those around them, but unfortunately this isn't very help-ful. In 2015, one in 1 000 households told the national Victims of Crime Survey that there had been a murder of someone in their household in the past 12 months.[55] That would suggest a murder rate more than a hundred times higher than the num-bers recognised by the police, passing through mortuaries or confirmed through the census and vital registration. Surveys just don't make it possible to get a good sense of the preva-lence of crimes such as murder. For one thing, when it comes to such highly salient personal events as murders, people tend to radically underestimate how much time has passed since they happened.[56] They may report in a survey that their household has experienced a murder in the last year when in fact it hap-pened more than a year ago, or not in fact to someone in the direct household, such that these incidents can be hugely over-counted. We've already said that surveys are most useful for corroborating broad trends over time. As we will see in a later chapter, they have indeed confirmed the trends in the official murder figures.

In short, the modern SAPS murder figures are not perfect. They are likely to be an undercount. But the evidence suggests that the undercount is probably quite small in most places. The overall magnitude, distribution and trend in the SAPS mur-der figures are all corroborated by other sources. National and international experts alike have no particular concerns about the accuracy of the modern South African homicide rate. While keeping in mind that the exact numbers are not entirely accurate, there is no good reason to reject them as a solid basis of tracking and comparison.

The population problem

A further difficulty in making sense of crime figures is that jurisdictions vary in size. Comparing the number of crime figures recorded by the police in China with those of the Seychelles would be absurd without taking into account that one country has about 15 000 times more people than the other. Similarly, regardless of recording, policing, demographic and social dynamics, it would be surprising if South Africa didn't have more crime incidents this year than it did a century ago, when it had a population of about a tenth as many people. It would also be surprising if there wasn't more crime in a big city centre thronging with hundreds of thousands than on the main street of a small town, even though each may be served by just one police station.

For this reason, while the raw number of crimes reported in an area is certainly institutionally useful for planning the distribution of resources, when it comes to analysis of trends over time or comparisons between places, it is standard to divide the number of crimes reported by the number of people in the area. The international norm is to express the recorded crime figures as rates per 100 000 people in the population (although sometimes for smaller places or less common crimes the rate is instead given per 10 000 or even per 1 000 people). Appropriately, in addition to raw figures, the SAPS has for over 20 years released its national and provincial crime statistics as rates per 100 000. This goes a long way to making different places and times comparable in terms of average risk of crime victimisation, especially for crimes against persons such as murder or assault. But although the rate of cellphone theft per 100 000 people is many times higher today than it was 20 years ago, this probably doesn't mean that the average cellphone is many times more likely to be stolen, given how many more cellphones are now available for possible stealing. For crimes against objects, it would be more useful to compare the crime figure with how many of those objects there are in the population under consideration. So carjacking figures would ideally be given in proportion to the number of cars, house burglaries to the number of residences, stock theft to livestock numbers, etc. Unfortunately, it is generally impossible to get regular and reliable estimates of these numbers, so we are forced to make do with human population sizes.

Even getting reliable numbers for human population distributions can be difficult. Conducting a census, or an official count of the population, is a huge, intrusive and expensive task. The first modern scientific census in South Africa was conducted in the Cape of Good Hope in 1865, and the rest of the nineteenth century saw a number of others there and elsewhere, but they were irregular, had unsystematic coverage and were usually only concerned with the white population.[57] Ostensibly national censuses began after the formation of the Union of South Africa in 1910, and followed at intervals of roughly 5, 10 or 15 years thereafter. Racial and language classification and regulation, international and internal migration, and the extent of the franchise all played key roles in these events, and the results were politically powerful.[58] Where and in what numbers people of different races lived became increasingly fraught questions. The issue of the Bantustans meant that the Pretoria-recognised national borders and population saw numerous changes from the 1970s, and by the 1980s there were also areas in 'white' South Africa considered too dangerous for enumerators to go. As a result, South African population estimates prior to 1996 are erratic and of poor quality. To compound the problem, the SAP's understanding of its jurisdiction – and therefore the official reach of its crime figures – may not have corresponded with the borders as understood by the Department of Statistics or Central Statistical Service (predecessors to Statistics South Africa).

As of the first post-apartheid national census, in 1996, most of these distortions are no longer at play. However, a census remains a task so large and complicated that it can only happen every few years, and a range of assumptions and variables go into generating official population estimates for the years in between. They can get it wrong. After the most recent census, in 2011, it was discovered that the country's population had been growing faster than had been estimated since the previous census, of 2001, and was at 52.3 million people rather than the 50.6 million that had been forecast. This meant that the population estimates that the SAPS (and everyone else, due to no fault of their own) had been using for the previous decade's crime rate calculations had become increasingly inaccurate. As of 2012/2013, the SAPS proceeded correctly to use the new, larger population number for the denominator in its simple crime rate calculations. But the population did not grow by 1.7 million in the course of one year. To get an accurate sense of the trend over time, it would have been necessary to recalculate the crime rates of the past ten years with revised historical population estimates. The Institute for Security Studies called for them to do so, and even for an independent inquiry to be established to investigate the fact that they had not.[59] The SAPS declined, claiming that it was not its practice to revise historical rates, that it would just confuse people, and essentially that this is just a slight hiccough that should be expected around census years.[60] We have done what the SAPS has not. For the rest of this book, we use the historical population figures as revised by Statistics South Africa following the 2011 census. The crime trends we demonstrate are based on the raw crime figures exactly as provided in each relevant year by the SAPS, but represent more accurate crime rates per 100 000 for the years to 2012/2013.

Perhaps because it didn't wish to reopen this debate, in the latest release of 2014/2015 the SAPS did not provide rates at all. This is highly irregular and makes it difficult to make

The impact of the rate recalculation

The significance of the revised population estimates for the crime rates is most easily demonstrated with an example. The murder rates for the last decade as provided by the SAPS, and as compared to the murder rate based on revised historical population estimates, can be seen in Figure 2.

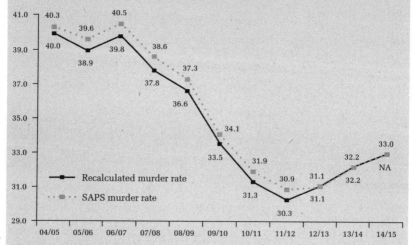

Figure 2: Comparison detail of murder rate from SAPS vs recalculation with corrected population estimates

The difference is relatively small (note the vertical axis scale), especially in the broad longitudinal view. However, given the SAPS practice of emphasising percentage changes between relatively arbitrary past dates and the present, the difference is significant. According to the SAPS rates calculation, the percentage change from the low point in 2011/2012 to 2014/2015 is an increase of 6.7 per cent. According to the recalculation, the increase is 9 per cent, or over a third larger than the SAPS result.

Because the SAPS crime rates prior to 2012/2013 were inflated by too-small population estimates, calculations of percentage increases since then in the SAPS rates are flattened, and decreases exaggerated. In other words, the reality of the change in the crime situation from before 2012/2013 to after is invariably slightly worse (or less good) than that suggested by the SAPS on the unrevised figures. This has contributed to the suspicion with which some have viewed its refusal to revise its historical crime rate calculations.

sense of trends in the context of population growth or of the differences between provinces. It also makes for a deceptively negative picture, as for example it must now be declared that the raw number of murders is 4.6 per cent higher in 2014/2015 than it was in 2013/2014, whereas taking population growth into account shows that the increase in the murder rate is only 2.3 per cent. The choice to effectively ignore population growth would seem to contradict the assumption that the SAPS would do everything in its power to present its performance in a positive light. Without taking account of provincial population estimates, we are also then left wondering what to make of the fact that in 2014/2015, 3 810 murders were recorded in KwaZulu-Natal whereas 413 were recorded in the Northern

Cape. It is to be hoped that the SAPS will reintroduce rates per 100 000 in future statistical releases.

Unfoundedness

The SAPS introduced one additional complication into its statistical release for 2014/2015. For the first time, it gave the total not for every charge laid, but rather for the number of cases not classified as 'unfounded'. According to the SAPS, a case is considered unfounded 'when it is evident from the investigation that no offence has been committed. For example, when it is alleged that goods have been stolen and the investigation proves that the goods were merely misplaced, the docket is closed as unfounded/false/civil matter.'[61] The figures are therefore slightly smaller than they would have been had this change not been made. Excluding the unfounded cases from the released crime figures gives arguably a more accurate view of the prevalence of crime. On the other hand, it introduces greater scope for police discretion in determining the statistics. Comparing the two sets of figures for the years for which we have comparable data, it is clear that for most crimes the difference is negligible – usually less than half a per cent.

Only for six crime types is the average difference greater than one per cent: stock theft (10 per cent), arson (5.9 per cent), commercial crime (3.1 per cent), malicious injury to property (1.9 per cent), all theft not mentioned elsewhere (1.8 per cent) and total sexual offences (1.8 per cent). The SAPS has noted that the significant proportion of unfounded stock theft cases is due to mismanagement of stock, with lost or stray animals often erroneously being reported as stolen.[62] Fair enough. For arson and malicious damage to property, SAPS docket analysis has suggested that these (as well as assault) tend to cluster together, usually involve interpersonal or intergroup conflicts in private or social spaces, and are often fuelled by alcohol and drugs – typically, they involve an argument in a bar, tavern, shebeen or home, devolving into a physical fight and damage to the surrounding property.[63] The relatively high proportion of these cases considered unfounded may be due to the chaotic nature of such events, to possibly spurious charges being laid by various aggrieved participants,[64] or to property owners wishing to make false insurance claims.[65] All theft not mentioned elsewhere (which excludes the major named forms such as theft of or out of vehicles, break-ins and stock theft) and commercial crime may also see relatively high rates of unfoundedness because of false insurance claims,[66] because of difficulties in detection[67] or because many items may turn out to have been lost rather than stolen.[68]

More worrying is the fact that for the six years for which there is comparable data, the rate of police-determined unfoundedness in sexual offences varied between 1.5 and 2 per cent of the cases. There are inevitably a series of attrition points in the criminal justice process, but for sexual crimes a great deal of evidence suggests that a large number never make it past the first point and into the charge office, and that the second point – the police decision whether to open the gateway to the criminal justice system by opening a docket – is also a major hurdle, with considerable scope for abuse and injustice.[69] As such, the fact that there is also significant attrition at the third point, where police undertake some investigation and conclude whether the evidence suggests that an offence has been committed, is cause for concern. Bringing more of officers' discretion about sexual crimes, which may reflect ingrained beliefs about the credibility of complainants, can further compromise the already extremely limited accuracy of official statistics on such crimes.

It slightly complicates comparison over time that the released crime statistics changed in 2014/2015 from reflecting all charges laid to only those not deemed unfounded. Although the SAPS has provided comparable figures for the previous nine years, it has not done so for the years prior to that. In order to distort the recent trend as little as possible, we have opted here to use the unfounded figures as provided by the SAPS from 2005/2006, but for years prior to that must use the full number of charges recorded by the police. The differences, largely of less than half a per cent, are negligible in the context of the long-term trend, which we think is the most interesting and valuable perspective on many of the crime statistics.

• • •

The annual round of quips, doubts and accusations around the release of the new crime statistics is probably to a large extent politically inevitable. What they needn't be is quite so opaque. The uncertainties are considerable, but we can only begin to try to mitigate them or appropriately account for them in the nature or confidence of our conclusions when they're clearly laid out on the table. As the last two chapters have shown, there are plenty of reasons to be wary of the official crime statistics. Some of them are inherent to the nature of this kind of data, and some to the history of the South African state's relationship with its population. The scales of the confounding factors are why experts, practitioners and politicians often make a point of referring to the problems with the 'validity' of the crime statistics. Changes in law, policing approach, data capacity, police-community relations and other social factors have been and will probably continue to be larger and more rapid than those in more stable places in the world, which tend also to be those with lower crime rates. Having gained a basic understanding of what the crime statistics can't do and exactly why, we can finally begin exploring what they legitimately can reveal about where South Africa fits into the world. It is to this that we turn in the next chapter.

3

Headline international comparison

A sense of how South Africa compares globally in terms of safety is a key factor in how many people think and talk about this country. It influences choices as small as what to tell visitors and as momentous as whether to uproot whole families and move them abroad. Comparisons are invoked in conversations on anything remotely political. Terms like 'crime capital', 'murder capital' and 'warzone' crop up often. As does talk of our position on 'the global rankings'.

But for reasons that should already be becoming clear, determining the 'true' measure of crime in just one time and place has been described as like searching for the Holy Grail.[1] The problem is further complicated by the difficulty of obtaining defensible, comparable estimates for many places, and by the difficulties of making valid criminological comparisons.

Crime isn't standardised, and there is no regular event where countries compete under controlled circumstances to prove who's safer. Places invariably differ in a host of respects, such that, for example, one widely respected attempt to rank countries by their level of 'peace' takes into account 15 key indicators, including military expenditure, incarceration numbers, the size of the small arms industry and economic losses due to refugees.[2] On that ranking, South Africa in 2015 comes in 136th out of 162 countries – in the 'low' category, but not 'very low'.[3] Countries that score worse include the Philippines, India, Mexico, Israel, Russia and Syria. This may not be a ranking system that resonates with what many people think of as 'crime'. The problem is that to capture any level of complexity, the task of comparison must involve a range of decisions about how to weight different potential factors.

Should the title of 'crime capital' go to the country with the most child abuse, the highest value of thefts, the lowest conviction rates, the most spending on private security, the greatest fear of crime or some combination of these factors and others? Where is the line between lawbreaking that is criminal and that which is political? Should mass deaths due to terrorism be categorised together with interpersonal murder? Should gender-selective abortion or infanticide? What about transgressions of laws in places that are undemocratic and have little respect for human rights? What should we make of the observation that countries with relatively strong gender equality may have among the highest recorded rates of gender-based crimes? Should we think of a country as becoming more or less criminal when people fall foul of a good new law? What if in one country the crime is evenly distributed, but in another it is highly concentrated in a few areas? What if one has more violence against men but another has more against women and children? What if people in one are more afraid of crime, while those in the other are at greater real risk of victimisation? Does it make sense to compare countries that are highly industrialised with those that are largely based on subsistence living? How do we take account of the fact that the accuracy of all the necessary figures may be much higher in the relatively stable places than in the more chaotic? How do we weight the experiences and opinions of different sectors of society – the poor, the elite, business leaders, the police, academic experts, and so on? There are no easy answers and there are many defensible ways one might go about making a global ranking of crime or safety.

Given all these difficulties, comparative crime researchers have developed a short-cut. It is widely accepted to be imperfect but nevertheless probably the simplest way to get some measure of the extent and seriousness of criminality in a given place and time. It requires only two pieces of information, just two numbers: the best guess for the size of the population and the best guess for the number of murders or homicides that happened in the last year. We've said previously that murder figures are the gold standard of crime statistics. Murder

is relatively clear and consistent in legal and casual definition, its extent is relatively well and consistently captured in
official statistics, and it is subject to confirmation from other
sources.

Although it is rare compared to most other crimes, murder
is a lightning rod of public concern and it is often considered a
strong indicator of crime and violence more generally, in both
lay and scholarly thinking.[4] The relationship isn't perfect, but
it is broadly agreed that murder figures provide a fairly solid basis for conclusions about overall levels of safety.[5] Places
and times with more murders tend to be places and times with
more other criminal rule-breaking. Places and times with more
murders per capita probably correspond with what many people think of as ones that are 'more criminal'. Therefore, the
majority of research that seeks to compare different countries
or track crime levels over a long period does so by the simple
metric of murder figures as a proportion of the total population,
even though patterns might look quite different for other, especially non-violent, crimes.

In their crime statistics release of September 2015, the SAPS
reported its knowledge of 17 805 murders nationally between
1 April 2014 and 31 March 2015. That's about 49 a day. Statistics
South Africa estimated that in mid-2014 there were just over
54 million people in the country.[6] That makes for an annual
national murder rate of about 0.033 per cent, meaning that the
average person in the country had a one in a little over 3 000
chance of being murdered in the year. Or, as it is generally

expressed, 33 out of every 100 000 people in the country were murdered in 2014/2015. We should try to get a sense of how that compares.

Where South Africa fits in

For most of its history, the world was far more violent than it is today.[7] A number of social and political processes over the centuries have radically reduced levels of violence in places that have relatively established states and relatively high levels of something we might call 'development'. Large swathes of the world that we now consider very safe once saw levels of violence that dwarf those in all but a handful of the worst places today. One of the first systematic attempts to collate crime data from many countries was made by Interpol, the international police co-operation agency, which collected and (with no quality control) published the data provided by its member countries every two years from 1950,[8] and every year from 1993, until they stopped making public releases in 1999.[9] The most complete, rigorous and up-to-date database on global murder rates now is that compiled by the United Nations Office on Drugs and Crime (UNODC). According to that, the global murder rate is currently about 6 per 100 000, and although there is no objective benchmark of what number is too high when it comes to violent deaths, on the global scale murder rates are often called high when above 20 per 100 000, and very high when above 30.[10] The SAPS murder figure for 2014/2015 makes for a murder rate of 33 per 100 000. With about 0.7 per cent of the world's population, we account for about 3.7 per cent of its recorded murders.[11] The average person in South Africa is five times more likely to be murdered than the average person in the world.

The UNODC dataset has been rightly criticised in the past for its major omissions,[12] but it has improved considerably in recent years, to the point where it now covers all 193 United Nations member states as well as 26 territories or autonomous entities, such as Hong Kong and the respective US and UK Virgin Islands. It sources its data from either criminal justice or public health systems as submitted by the relevant member states, taken from public data sources, or as estimated by other bodies such the World Health Organization.[13] It also attempts to standardise and validate definitions and methods wherever possible, and conducts consultations with member states to this end.[14]

But the quality of the data collected remains highly variable. While most countries in Europe, the Americas and Asia have national data repositories of either or both criminal justice and public health figures, many in Africa and Oceania do not have them at all or of passable coverage. As a result, the homicide rates provided for these latter countries are estimates based on a standardised statistical model, which are probably not meaningfully comparable to data from the national administration systems elsewhere. There also remain some differences in definition that confound direct

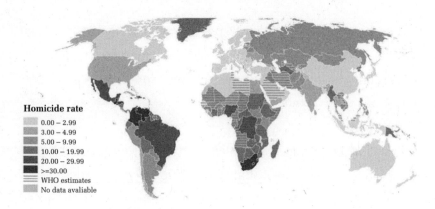

Homicide rate
- 0.00 – 2.99
- 3.00 – 4.99
- 5.00 – 9.99
- 10.00 – 19.99
- 20.00 – 29.99
- >=30.00
- WHO estimates
- No data avaliable

Figure 3: Homicide rates, by country or territory (2012 or latest year), from UNODC Global Study on Homicide, 2013

comparison. Although most countries do have a distinct legal category corresponding to what the UNODC terms 'intentional homicide', which in South Africa is called 'murder', some countries include in that category killings out of self-defence, or may, for example, keep separate account of infanticides.[15] Many regional and international initiatives are in place to try progressively to improve and standardise all this data.[16] In recognition of all these factors, the UNODC tends to stress patterns and trends within countries and regions, providing contextual information about the local drivers of violence and, for example, the dynamics of gender and weapon availability. They do not themselves create a ranking of individual countries. Their most explicit global comparison is in the form of a map, as shown in Figure 3.[17]

However, keeping clearly in mind that the chief international collector and analyst of murder rates avoids directly comparing

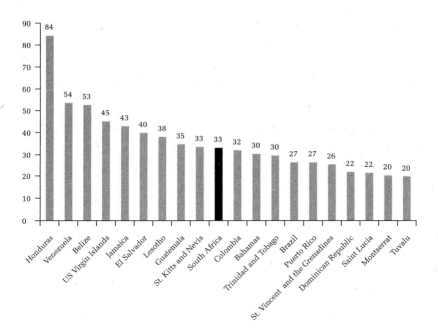

Figure 4: National murder rates above 20 per 100 000 in most recent year on record

them, we can extract from their dataset the top 20 countries or territories by murder rate in the most recent year for which it has figures.[18] These also happen to be the only ones with their latest murder rates above 20 per 100 000. This ranking of what we can call the current '20 above 20' is indicated in Figure 4.

By this account, South Africa's murder rate in 2014/2015 puts it solidly in the top 20 countries or territories by murder rate, currently at about 10th place in the world. Whether that justifies the title of 'capital' is a matter of personal judgement, but certainly it is a worse position than the vast majority of places in the world. This is just a snapshot at one point in time. Some

85

of those on this list are seeing murder rates this high following a number of years of rise, others after declines or in the context of erratic fluctuation. Other data sources, methodologies and years' data would result in a different line-up, but the top ranks of murder in the recent past are by most accounts dominated by Central and South America, the Caribbean and southern Africa.

It cannot be overemphasised that the value of such a ranking is determined by the quality of the data on which it is based, and we know that this is seriously compromised in exactly those places that are relatively chaotic and may well have high levels of violence. It may be perplexing, for example, that the countries with listed murder rates below the European average of 3 per 100 000 include Bangladesh and Libya, that South Africa's murder rate is three times that of Nigeria and almost six times that of Somalia, which in turn is only four times that of Canada. In places like Venezuela, it may be almost impossible to get to a satisfactory level of accuracy, as the differences in estimates from different sources (for example, the health system, the judicial system or nongovernmental organisations) are so large and politicised.[19] Some countries (South Africa not among them) are suspected by experts of significantly manipulating their official murder rates in order to avoid being seen in an unfavourable light.[20] Some differences in murder rates may less reflect levels of criminal disorder than differences in the lethality of violence, which may come down to access to and quality of medical care.[21] All told, and to say the least, the enthusiasm for neat international crime level comparison on the part of the media and politicians is seldom shared by experts.[22] Many reject the entire project as at the least deceptively precise, at the most hopelessly flawed.[23]

Even without placing much stock in the precise numbers, however, it does seem that South Africa has extremely high levels of serious crime. By the best measure we have, they are among the highest in the world. To turn this observation into something more practically useful, we can reflect on what else we can make of this ranking.

Insight from the company we keep

There is no global consensus on the relative importance of the key factors that determine why some places have quite so much more crime and violence than others. The issue is not that there are no plausible theories and statistical clues, but that there are so many. Even the most cursory look at the countries that rank extremely high on murder rates, however, can give some insight into likely reasons, and especially whether it is surprising to find South Africa among them. First, they are mostly in the 'New World' or Western hemisphere, and what might be called 'developing' countries. Most are middle-income, none are low-income, and the handful that are high-income are small island states in the Caribbean.[24] Most have high levels of income inequality.[25] Most have some manner of democracy, but few have had long periods of political stability, or are without what are considered major democratic flaws.[26] A number have seen civil war, coup d'état, dictatorship or some form of major political violence within living memory. None of this is the least surprising.

As the reach and quality of international data has improved in recent years, we have come ever closer to untangling what sets the countries with high crime rates apart from others. A large amount of research has shown that variations in murder rates between countries are principally determined by some combination of concentrated poverty, inequality and (probably to a lesser degree)[27] economic development.[28] Concentrations of these factors make acquisitive crime more attractive, raise levels of frustration and weaken communities' capacity to regulate the behaviour of their young people.[29] These all raise levels of crime and violence. Inequality in particular is highly socially corrosive, as it lowers levels of trust and community engagement, and raises levels of hostility.[30] Inequality has an especially strong impact on violent crime when it is highly visible,[31] including when that visibility takes the form of race.[32] The importance of inequality is one reason why the countries with the highest rates of murder are not the poorest, least developed ones, but the ones that contain both poverty and obvious development and wealth. True, there are some countries with murder rates either higher or lower than that predicted by these socioeconomic factors alone. In these places, there are strong mitigating or aggravating variables to consider – such as cultural factors, the strength of organised crime[33] or the particular influence of alcohol and other drugs and/or their prohibition.[34] There are also dynamics that can have considerable bearing on changes in the murder rates within countries over time. But places with high levels of inequality, especially if they also contain high levels of poverty, are overwhelmingly likely to have high levels of violent crime, according to a number of data sources and for different measures of violent crime.[35]

It is crucial to note already at this stage that the concentration of wealth does not raise levels of violence evenly within a country. Neither does it result primarily in violence committed across the divide between the have-littles and have-lots. Quite the contrary, violence (as well as a range of other harmful life and health outcomes such as accidental injury and infant mortality) concentrates heavily in the same places within a country and within a city where poverty concentrates.[36] There is some spillover in violence, more so in property crime, but it is limited. It is not that inequality drives the poor to eat the rich; it is overwhelmingly the poor who eat each other. We will return to this and demonstrate its implications for the South African context in the next chapter. Moreover, rational calculation of enrichment plays little role in the majority of violence in South Africa, which mostly generates little or no material reward for its participants.[37] We will also return to the question of the character of violence in a later chapter.

Another robust finding of comparative research is that new, poorly consolidated, modernising democracies have high levels of violent crime.[38] The disruption of traditional social order, even in ways that are desirable and necessary to achieve long-term goals, raises levels of crime and violence.[39] Political upheaval undermines social structures and state capacity. It also undermines state legitimacy, another key determinant of levels of crime and violence.[40] Stability, accountability and trust in the relationship between state and society reproduce peace over the long term.[41] From the level of the family all the way through to the nation, violence reproduces violence.[42] High-violence countries have recent histories of major political conflict, officially approved violence and disrupted systems of social control.[43]

Countries' murder rates can with a high degree of accuracy be predicted by their concentrations of poverty and levels of inequality, and beyond that by their recent histories and patterns of social instability and political violence. There may well, of course, be a mutually reinforcing or other complex relationship between these factors, but there is no doubt that they are some of the strongest international determinants of crime and violence.[44] The crime statistics show that violent societies are overwhelmingly likely to be the ones that are unequal, fractured, disrupted and traumatised.

South Africa has perhaps the single highest level of income inequality in the world.[45] It has large, concentrated pools of poverty and structural exclusion, plus small islands of comfort and wealth. It is barely less true now than it was when Deputy President Thabo Mbeki said in 1998 that this is a country of two nations, with one experiencing conditions of human development akin to Zimbabwe or Swaziland, and the other like those in Israel or Italy.[46] There has since 1994 been improvement in the non-monetary wellbeing of many, and some reduction in the interracial income gap, but the country remains acutely socioeconomically and spatially stratified.[47] The boundaries are conspicuous and barely less practically rigid than before, still overlapping closely with apartheid's legal categories of 'race'.[48] Comparing international crime statistics indicates that these are extremely powerful drivers of crime and violence. South Africa is not among those countries with crime rates other than as predicted by their socioeconomic mix.[49] In other words, if we knew nothing about the country but its current socioeconomic profile, we could predict that it would have extremely high levels of violence. There is more.

Within the last century, South Africa has gone from an overwhelmingly rural to a majority urban profile.[50] Within living memory, millions of South Africans had their lives entirely uprooted by being forcibly removed from their homes and relocated to areas far from jobs, with poor infrastructure, chronic overcrowding, insecure tenure and devastated systems of community control and socialisation. Even when not dislocated through active state force, many families were driven by the demands of the labour market into precarious, migrant, divided lives. Within even more recent history, some areas were embroiled in what was in effect a low-grade civil war. For the vast majority of the country, relations with the state have until recently been characterised not by accountability or trust, but instead by humiliation, indignity and violent confrontation. This is certainly not unique among African colonial administrations, but no other African country had the industrial and infrastructural power to so enforce its will and to imprison its subjects on anything like the same scale.[51] If we knew nothing about South Africa but its social and political history during the twentieth century, we could probably predict that it would have high levels of violence.

It has been said that an important cultural feature of the American poor is that they see themselves as temporarily embarrassed millionaires.[52] It has also been said that South African criminologists and citizens alike were taken by surprise and have struggled to come to terms with the failure of the advent of democratic governance to reduce national levels of violence to less extreme levels.[53] If this last is so, one can only conclude that South Africa must somehow see itself as a temporarily embarrassed Sweden. For all that relatively privileged South Africans may culturally identify with and live lifestyles akin to those in the wealthy old democracies of the developed world, the history and socioeconomic structure of this country is entirely unlike theirs. In the ways that the statistics show us are important, South Africa today is exactly like the other countries with high levels of violence and fundamentally unlike the countries with low levels of violence. There is no mystery at all as to why post-apartheid South Africa is among the most violent places in the world. It has followed the simple recipe to the letter, and added aggravating seasoning to taste, in the form, for example, of the relatively easy availability of firearms, a social pattern of binge drinking, a sophisticated apparatus for promoting consumerist values and an attractive regional launch point for organised crime and drugs.[54] South African exceptionalism does not extend to the negation of some of the most established laws of social and economic cause and effect.

The trouble with other crimes

For non-fatal violent crime or for property crime, international comparison is almost impossible. Definitions and reporting rates vary too much. There is some overlap between the countries (and smaller areas like cities) with high recorded rates of murder and those with high recorded rates of, say, robbery, but there are even more exceptions. For example, with about 3 per cent the murder rate, the United Kingdom has a slightly higher recorded robbery rate than the Bahamas.[55] Denmark and New Zealand both have higher recorded house burglary rates than South Africa.[56] The problem with making any sense of these figures is that people's relationships with the police and their ideas and incentives around reporting differ a great deal and are not independent of how much crime they experience. Only about half of South Africa's burglaries get reported to the police,[57] whereas reporting rates in Denmark are among the highest in the world.[58] Recorded rates of crimes other than murder are simply not usefully comparable between countries.

Victimisation surveys can help a bit. Data from international victimisation surveys indicate that both robbery and burglary rates tend to be higher in developing countries than in developed ones, and track much better with murder rates than their official recorded figures would suggest.[59] But there are also many differences, with residents in some countries reporting victimisation rates above average for burglary but below average for robbery, with no clear relationship to their murder rates.[60] Standardised international victimisation surveys are also infrequent, especially in the developing world (the most recent results for many countries are more than a decade old), where they also seldom have national coverage. To the extent that we can extrapolate from such imperfect and outdated sources, it seems likely that South Africa has rates of robbery that are far higher than the developed-country average and slightly lower than in some developing countries,[61] and rates of burglary somewhat higher than in the former and more mixed in terms of the latter.[62] We do not have the means to defensibly quantify the extent of those disparities. In national surveys, self-reported victimisation rates of burglary in South Africa for the year to March 2015 were about 5 per cent,[63] as compared to about 2.3 per cent in the US,[64] and about 2.7 per cent in the UK,[65] but these national surveys are not standardised and don't ask their questions in identical ways. Based on self-reported victimisation, many other African countries with much lower murder rates seem to have much higher rates of burglary than South Africa.[66] On the other hand, South Africans seem to be far more afraid of crime in their home than those African countries with greater victimisation, which may suggest that circumstances around the crimes may be different.[67]

Experiences of crime vary by far more factors than simply how frequent they are in a population, which is one of the reasons why victimisation surveys are not all that useful for revealing the absolute level of crime. International comparison on the basis of self-reported victimisation rates may sometimes be slightly more helpful than officially recorded figures, but not by much. They also seldom disaggregate to small enough areas to be useful, given the highly uneven distribution of crime victimisation, which we'll describe in the next chapter.

• • •

Placing national crime statistics or self-reported victimisation rates in international perspective – viewing them in global cross-section – can provide not just an interesting sense of context, but can also make it possible to start narrowing down why things are as we observe them. This is where we need to start in figuring out what to do about them. What this level of analysis can't do is tell you very much about the risks faced by individuals. The fact that the murder rate in South Africa is 33 per 100 000 and that in the United States is about 4 per 100 000 *does not mean* that moving from the one to the other reduces a given person's risk of being murdered eightfold or, for example, that the diplomat deployed to Pretoria is at eight times the risk they were at in Washington, DC.[68] Because a major shortcoming so far is that we have effectively imagined the country as a single unit, with crime spread evenly among its inhabitants. This could not be further from the truth. The large differences in rates of crime between sub-national regions, cities, neighbourhoods and populations have fascinated social scientists for at least as long as they've had the numbers to describe them. Knowing how the South African national crime rate compares to the crime rate of another country is of extremely limited value in working out the actual risk faced by individuals. For that, we must dig deeper into the profound differences between the spaces and groups within the country.

4

Breaking down the numbers

There are some features that are shared and that spill across the various forms of boundaries, but the differences are vast between the crime patterns that play out in different parts of the country, in each city, in each neighbourhood and even in each household. Passing from one to another entirely distinct crime situation does not require a passport. Often, all it takes is a short walk. The national rates of crime are abstractions, based on averaging out and simplifying millions of experiences that, in their differences, can tell us a great deal more about the shapes of our lives and societies. The failure of the police and some commentators to consistently break the national crime picture down into the spatial units that matter in people's lives contributes to the disconnection between people's levels of risk and their levels of fear. The void of knowledge is easily filled with an abundance of rumour, anecdote and assumption. So it can be that it is common to hear Johannesburg described as the murder capital of the country, when it doesn't even have the highest murder rate in Gauteng, and in fact has among the lowest murder rates of any of the major cities. So, too, can it be that – in the context of sharp racial segregation by space – there are many people who seem genuinely to believe that the distribution of crime risk by racial group is precisely the reverse of what all the evidence suggests that it is.[1]

To make sense of what the crime statistics mean for individuals, it is necessary to narrow the geographic focus as much as possible. There are strengths and weakness at each level, but as we zoom in further with each step, it should become increasingly clear that the crime statistics can tell a far more complex and useful story than simply that the national murder rate is such-and-such.

The SAPS functions, manages and evaluates not just at the national level, but also at the level of province, area cluster (consisting usually of about half a dozen stations) and station. In addition to the national total, it also publicly releases the crime figures for each province and for each of over 1 000 police station precincts. To make it possible to compare places, we also need estimates of their population sizes. For the 2011 census the country was demarcated into over 100 000 tiny pieces of land called Enumeration Areas, each of which had clearly defined boundaries, had an average of 180 households and could be covered by one fieldworker during the count period.[2]

Enumeration Area data are bundled into slightly larger units known as Small Areas, which in turn group together into Sub Places, into Main Places, municipalities, districts or metros, provinces and finally the country as a whole. We have a count (and of course a range of other information) for the people in each of those levels on the night of 9 October 2011, as adjusted by Statistics South Africa for undercounting.

Provinces

In previous years, as we have indicated, the SAPS provided the provincial rates in the crime statistics release. As on the national level, it opted not to do so in 2014/2015. Luckily, creating provincial crime rates is a simple matter of dividing the number of crimes recorded in each province by the number of people estimated to live in that province (multiplied by 100 000, as is customary). Provincial crime rate comparison has the advantage that Statistics South Africa updates its provincial population estimates every year, by adjusting the census results by a range of factors. So with little difficulty we can determine that 2014/2015's national murder rate of 33 per 100 000 is roughly on par with the murder rate in Gauteng (28 per 100 000), the Free State (34), Northern Cape (35) and KwaZulu-Natal (36), but significantly overstates the average murder victimisation rate in the North West (23), Mpumalanga (20) and Limpopo (14), and understates that in the Eastern Cape (49) and the Western Cape (52).

If the provinces were countries, in 2014/2015 all but Limpopo would make it on to the list of countries/territories with murder rates above 20 per 100 000. So would a number of sub-national regions in other parts of the world. The average murder victimisation risk in the Western Cape is almost four times that in Limpopo. Large variation between sub-national regions is common. For example, the murder rate in the American state of Louisiana (10.3) is about ten times that in New Hampshire (0.9).[3] This means that the average resident of Limpopo is only marginally more likely to be murdered than the average resident of Louisiana, whereas the average resident of the Western Cape is almost 60 times more likely to be murdered than the average resident of New Hampshire.

We can also now start to see why murder is not a perfect proxy for other types of crime. Based on the recorded figures, it clearly is not the case that having more of one crime will mean that an area also has more of every other. Although the Eastern Cape has a relatively high rate of murder, it has a relatively low rate of car theft. The Northern Cape has by a good margin the highest rate of assault with intent to inflict grievous bodily harm, while Gauteng has a large lead in residential robbery. Recorded crime rates vary a good deal by province, and some provinces may lead in some crimes while lagging in others. Broadly where you are in a country makes a major difference to your crime risk profile.

But South Africa is large, and some of these provinces are larger than many countries or autonomous territories, including a number of those on that '20 over 20' list. Knowing about crime rates and trends for KwaZulu-Natal as a whole probably doesn't much extend our knowledge, as the crime situation in Durban may have less in common with that in the small KZN town of Mkuze than it does with Pretoria. Large cities tend to have more crime – not just absolutely but also relative to their population size – than smaller urban or rural spaces. This has been known for a very long time, and there are many theories about which are the key causal factors, for example the greater anonymity, financial returns to crime, proximity to inequality, attractions for already crime-prone people or levels of family disruption.[4] In the vast majority of countries, the highest murder rates are found in the most populous cities.[5]

Cities

Comparisons involving cities in South Africa are unfortunately complicated by the fact that municipal boundaries aren't relevant to the SAPS organisational structure, so they haven't been matched up with the boundaries of police station precincts, and the SAPS doesn't provide crime figures on the city level. Even in places in the world where this isn't the case, the question of city crime rates is seldom as simple as it is for larger areas, especially as there is often some room for disagreement about which exactly are the most appropriate city boundaries. Because policing isn't governed by cities, however, in South Africa it takes quite a bit of work to pull the city numbers into a useful shape.

Extracting city crime statistics

The municipal boundaries and the police station boundaries do not perfectly overlap, but the two sets of spatial information are publicly available and the discrepancies between them can be determined with the help of geographic information system (GIS) technology.[6] Thus one can create lists of those station precincts whose boundaries overlap with the relevant municipal boundaries. We decided to include on the lists only those stations with 50 per cent or more of their area falling within the relevant municipal limits. The resulting lists may therefore in a handful of cases be counterintuitive; for example, if the station house is beyond the city boundaries but it is included here, or vice versa. Next, the crime figures for all the relevant stations were summed to create raw figure totals for each municipality for each recorded crime type for each of the last ten years.

To make the raw crime figure totals comparable between municipalities of varying size, it is necessary to determine the number of people resident within the same area covered by the crime figures (i.e. the area covered by all those stations with more than 50 per cent of their precincts within the relevant municipal boundaries). GIS technology was used to overlay the precinct boundaries with the Small Area level boundaries used by Statistics South Africa for Census 2011. These Small Areas are associated with headcounts from the census, making it possible to create a population estimate for each precinct. The headcounts for the precincts were then summed to create a total population figure for each municipality.

To account for population growth, this sum was then adjusted from its 2011 total based on whole city population growth estimates, also from Statistics South Africa.[7] Finally, the municipal raw crime figure totals were divided by the appropriate year's municipal population estimates to create rates per 100 000.

Having extracted the municipal crime and population rates, we can get a sense of the urban bias of crime. About 40 per cent of the people in the country live in one of the eight metropolitan municipalities of the City of Johannesburg, City of Cape Town, eThekwini (with its seat in Durban), Ekurhuleni (Germiston), City of Tshwane (Pretoria), Nelson Mandela Bay (Port Elizabeth), Buffalo City (East London) and Mangaung (Bloemfontein). For most crime types, these areas see considerably more than 40 per cent of the total reported nationally. Whereas the national murder rate in 2014/2015 was about 33 per 100 000, that in the metros combined was about 40. The discrepancies are particularly large for vehicle crimes and robbery, smaller for burglaries, and nearly zero or even slightly reversed for serious assault and sexual offences. Only in stock theft, unsurprisingly, do the metros lag behind the rest of the country. This pattern is not universal, but neither is it uncommon. In fact, it broadly matches that observed in one of the oldest studies on crime distribution. When the earliest French crime statistics were broken down by subregion, they showed that violent crime was highest in poorer rural areas while property crime was highest in wealthy, industrialised areas.[8] Although urban contexts get much of the focus, some conflict and post-conflict societies today also experience relatively high rates of violence in rural areas.[9]

Some of the urban bias in the recorded rates of crime may well be due to reporting factors (for example, as long distances to stations discourage reporting of less serious crimes), but although perhaps not to this extent, most crimes are probably genuinely more common in urban environments. This means that the relative risks of victimisation between people in two countries depends on whether they live in an urban or rural area.

Just as urban spaces differ from rural, cities within one country are also very different from each other. We can compare the murder rates in each of the major South African metros, as shown in Figure 5.

Whereas the City of Johannesburg's murder rate nearly matches the national rate, the City of Cape Town's murder rate is far higher, and the City of Tshwane far lower, with the other cities somewhere in between. The average person in Tshwane is about half as likely to be murdered as the average person in Mangaung, and about a third as likely as the average in Cape Town. There is no full and authoritative listing of murder rates for every city in the world, but by the standards of those for which we do have figures, some of these numbers are very high, with Cape Town in particular surpassed only by a few cities in Central and Latin America.[10] On the other hand, some

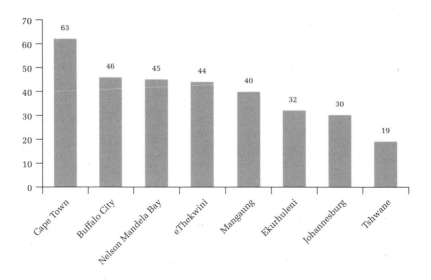

Figure 5: City murder rates by our calculations, 2014/2015

countries with relatively low national murder rates have city murder rates in this ballpark. The US national rate, and that in New York, were both about 4 per 100 000 in 2014, but rates were far higher in the cities of St Louis (50), Detroit (44) or New Orleans (39).[11] The average resident of Tshwane is only marginally less safe than the average resident of Washington, DC (16). The average resident of most South African cities is safer than the average resident in some cities in countries with far lower national murder rates.

A look at other crime categories further reveals that it is not simply the case that some cities have 'more crime' than others; their recorded crime patterns are different, with some crimes more common even as others are rarer from one city to another. Johannesburg leads in residential robbery, but lags in residential burglary. Mangaung has among the lowest rates of the former and among the highest of the latter. Based on the recorded figures, the average resident of each of these cities faces a completely different crime risk profile to the average resident in every other city. We showed in the previous chapter why international comparison for crimes other than murder is so difficult, but note here only that there are many cities in the US with rates of residential burglary more than twice that in the highest-ranked city in South Africa.[12] Even now we have not gone far enough in disaggregating the crime figures, because on no level is the distribution of crime as skewed as within each city.

Precincts

Here we begin to run into more difficulties – or rather the general difficulties become more acute the more thinly we slice the numbers. One problem is that the census count may not be accurate to begin with, especially in very densely populated places with a lot of informal housing. For example, the recent Khayelitsha Commission of Inquiry in Cape Town considered a number of 'sharply different' figures for the number of people in Khayelitsha,[13] including one about twice that estimated from the 2011 census, but it ultimately concluded that the census figures should be accepted as substantially accurate.[14] It is conceivable that there are areas where they should not, but there is as yet no more reliable and consistent alternative data source for the country. A second problem is that people move and places change. Although the census may have substantially accurately captured the number of people who slept in each area on that one night in October 2011, there may well be significantly more people sleeping there tonight, and many of the people who sleep there may in fact spend much of their time somewhere else. The census only happens every few years, so in the years between we can only guess at population changes in a precinct based on what was tracked between the last two censuses, or perhaps piece it together from other incomplete sources such as numbers of registered voters or grant recipients.

Besides confounding neighbourhood population estimates over time by moving, dying and multiplying, people are also of course highly mobile, and routinely experience and report crimes in places some distance from where they sleep. If you live in a major city, you may well pass through a dozen different precincts in a single ordinary day. Places with large daily influxes of commuters will see recorded crimes well out of proportion to the population estimated as resident there. For example, the station with by far the highest recorded rate of general theft in eThekwini municipality is that at King Shaka International Airport. This does not itself suggest that you're far more likely to have your items stolen at the airport than anywhere else in town. Not only does it host a daily flow of people vastly larger than the fewer than 200 people resident within the precinct boundaries, but it is also likely that many people on their way through stop at this station to report theft (or loss/damage purported for insurance purposes to be theft) that in fact happened elsewhere.[15] Comparing precinct-level crime rates is certainly an improvement on simply comparing precinct-level crime figures, but because the population in an area can change a great deal between different years, times of the year, week or even day, the comparison must still be done with considerable nuance and care.

Another problem is that for crimes other than murder, discretion in reporting may distort the results within a city considerably. Age, gender and socioeconomic factors play a major role in decisions to report crimes to the police.[16] Police discretion about where to focus resources may also distort the results, for example as more regular patrols may catch more criminals in the act. But as long as neighbourhood crime figures and rates are understood not as hard measurements of how much crime is happening but rather as broad indications of how recorded crime levels are distributed, to be supplemented with other knowledge about the character of the spaces, they are one of the most crucial and relatable tools for getting to grips with where crime happens.

Every city in the world has a skewed distribution of crime, usually with a small number of neighbourhoods recording rates well above the average, and most of them below. In the 1920s and 1930s, the city of Chicago gave birth to a now-large body of research and theory about why some neighbourhoods have so much more crime than others. What they found was that some measure of local economic disadvantage or deprivation accounted for most of the variation. Poorer areas generally have higher levels of violent crime than wealthier ones. Although much of the research still has an American focus,[17] a strong association between neighbourhoods' concentrations of disadvantage and their rates of violence has been found in cities all over the world, including places with relatively low levels of overall violence (such as Toronto,[18] the Netherlands,[19] cities in Western Europe,[20] London[21] and Stockholm[22]) and ones with very high levels of violence (like São Paulo,[23] Rio de Janeiro[24] and Kingston[25]). The relationship appears to be non-linear, such that extremely disadvantaged neighbourhoods have a lot more violence than moderately disadvantaged ones, although there is also the possibility that beyond a certain level of disadvantage, things can't really get worse.[26] There is some difficulty in isolating the precise mechanisms at play, because the common indicators of structural conditions (such as poverty, inequality, population heterogeneity and high population turnover) are often highly correlated,[27] and certainly other factors like police legitimacy and cultural frames can play a part.[28] The social and economic factors and the crime with which they are associated may also spill over into neighbouring areas in different ways.[29] Nevertheless, there is little doubt that concentrations of disadvantage are associated with concentrations of violent crime.[30]

The case for property crime is a little more complicated. The classic economic theory of crime suggests that the rich are highly attractive targets for property crimes, especially in conditions of high income inequality, but also that their relative capacity to invest in security can result in variation in their scope for crime avoidance.[31] In simpler terms, the relatively wealthy are targeted for property crime because they have more property worth stealing, but they may to varying degrees be able to protect themselves from that risk. Middle- and high-income households are often disproportionately targeted by property crime (in places with both generally high[32] and low[33] levels of crime), but, because of their relative wealth and the fact they often experience higher levels of fear of crime,[34] to some extent they compensate by investing in private security measures such as alarm systems and gated communities.[35] As a result, although violent crime is almost invariably concentrated among the economically vulnerable, and theft crimes often concentrate among the relatively wealthy,[36] the latter is to a lesser extent and its relationship is sometimes unclear or even for some crimes reversed.[37] So if in Figure 6, for example, we look at the three largest South African cities and sort their police precincts in declining order of murder rates, it is clear that the disparities in recorded crime rates are large and that they vary by type of crime. For the sake of scale, in eThekwini we exclude the outlier of King Shaka International Airport (because although its raw crime figures are very small, its miniscule residential population makes for extremely high rates) and the Maydon Wharf part of the harbour (because its recorded crime figures are negligible). The number of columns reflects the number of precincts in each city.

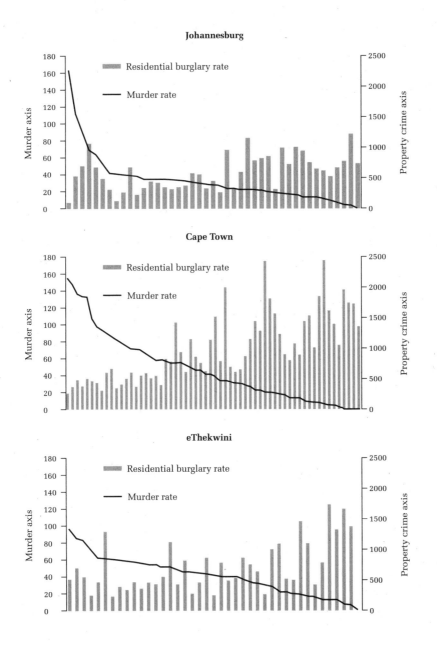

Figure 6: Precinct rates of selected crimes

In each of the three graphs in Figure 6 the left-hand side of the graph represents the precincts with the highest murder rates. In Johannesburg they reach a high of 166 per 100 000; in Cape Town, 155; in eThekwini, 97. To give a sense of the scale of this, the city that by some rankings is currently the most dangerous in the world, Caracas, Venezuela, is estimated to have a murder rate of 120 per 100 000.[38] The slopes of the murder rate lines show that murder is very highly concentrated in Johannesburg, less so in Cape Town, and even less so in eThekwini. To varying degrees, recorded residential burglary skews to the right.

In each, the left-hand side is dominated by areas that are less wealthy, while the right is dominated by wealthier suburbs. Other crimes peak in other places. There tend to be high rates of aggravated robbery recorded in places where there is a large daily commuter population and an unusual concentration of mobile items worth stealing – usually in busy business districts. In Cape Town, for example, the top two precincts by murder rate are Philippi East and Nyanga (in densely populated townships with large-scale poverty and informality); the top two by residential burglary are Claremont and Camps Bay (wealthy suburbs); and the top two by aggravated robbery are Cape Town Central and Parow (large business districts). In Johannesburg, the top two precincts in murder are Johannesburg Central (in the dense central business district) and Jeppe (a largely light industrial and commercial area with average household income about half the South African average); [39] the top in residential burglary are Linden and Florida (relatively wealthy suburbs), and the top in aggravated robbery are Johannesburg Central and Rosebank (business nodes). The recorded crime risk profile faced by the average resident in one part of the city is different from that faced by the average resident in another part of the same city.

Some of these differences for the crimes other than murder are almost certainly the result of reporting dynamics. Households in wealthier areas are more likely to be insured, and therefore to report all losses to the police. We do know that households in the Western Cape are considerably more likely to report burglary or robbery to the police than those in either Gauteng or KwaZulu-Natal.[40] The victimisation surveys do not disaggregate to a smaller level than the province and do not ask respondents to state their income level, so we can't determine exactly how these more local factors determine reporting rates. What we can do is draw some inferences from the questions that they do ask about race or population group.

The issue of the distribution of crime by race is a particularly fraught one in the South African context.[41] For example, there is in some spaces a mythology that whites are targeted for crime because of their race,[42] although the balance of available evidence suggests that racial hostility plays an extremely limited role in crime victim selection.[43] The old South African Police were fastidious in categorising crimes according to the legally designated racial groups of the victims and perpetrators. This is no longer the case, but we can look elsewhere to figure out how race informs crime victimisation patterns.

Note that we make use here of the language of the old apartheid racial classifications of black, coloured, Indian/Asian and white. In the interests of tracking progress towards eradicating the apartheid legacy and because they continue to hold so much socioeconomic salience, self-identification within these groups remains a common question in post-apartheid surveys.

Precisely because space, wealth and race still align fairly closely in much of the country, the spatial distribution of crime itself reveals a fair amount about racial distribution. We can often defensibly extrapolate some features about the victim on the basis just of where a crime happened. This isn't the case everywhere, though, and crucially it doesn't take account of differences in reporting rates.

Victimisation surveys have asked respondents to identify their population group, which makes it possible to disaggregate their results as follows. White respondents report experiencing rates of most violent or non-violent acquisitive crimes (including car theft, hijacking, residential burglary and robbery, and theft of personal property) above the national average and rates of interpersonal violent crimes (including assault and murder) below the national average.[44] Black respondents report experiencing relatively low rates for acquisitive crimes, but relatively high ones for murder and assault.[45] Coloured respondents' reported victimisation rates of most acquisitive crimes are generally below that for whites but above that for blacks, and they report rates well above any other population group for assault and robbery other than of house or car.[46] Indian/Asian respondents' self-reported rates are most similar to those of white respondents, with low rates of interpersonal violence crimes and high rates for acquisitive crimes.[47] Differences in rates of victimisation may not correspond with seriousness. For example, although white respondents are slightly more likely than average to report having been robbed, they are less likely to report having been injured during that robbery.[48] Reports for sexual offences in the national victimisation surveys are too low to make much sense of them for any population group. As for reporting, white respondents do appear to be the most likely to report their housebreaking (and almost all other crimes), followed by Indian/Asian, then coloured and then black respondents.[49]

The relationships between victimisation rates of violent crime are corroborated in mortuary figures, which suggest that, nationally, white people experience by far the lowest rates of murder, at about 11 per 100 000, followed by Indian/Asian people at 24, then black people at 41 and then coloured people at 43.[50] The pattern in non-metro areas appears to be slightly less skewed, with black and coloured people experiencing slightly lower rates of murder than their metro area counterparts, Indian/Asian people experiencing slightly higher rates, and no significant difference for white people.[51] This suggests that even at the lowest end of the national risk spectrum, white people in South Africa face murder risks far higher than the average residents of any major European city but below that in many in the US, including Chicago and Miami, and have a risk around that of the average resident of Houston, Texas. At the other end of the spectrum, coloured South Africans face risks around that of the average resident of Detroit.

The victimisation patterns in non-fatal violent crime and property crime suggested by victimisation survey results are harder to corroborate. There is some reason not to take them at entirely face value. That which people recount in a victimisation survey is not a perfect numerical record of the number of legal wrongs they have suffered in the period in question. Instead, it is a complex product of experience, perception, recollection, prioritisation and inclination to recount one particular subcategory of encounter to a stranger in the house. Victimisation is a subjective process, and as such its expression varies considerably.[52]

On the level of the neighbourhood, we can begin to make sense of the risks faced by different individuals, and how these risks compare to other places. Unfortunately, few cities usefully disaggregate their crime rates into smaller areas for this kind of comparison, but we can see some broad relationships. There are some parts of South African cities that have murder rates on par with some of the safest places in the world. Murder rates in suburbs like Rondebosch in Cape Town and Rosebank in Johannesburg would cause no concern if they were found in cities in Western Europe or Canada. Because its murder rates are extremely concentrated, about 90 per cent of the people who live in Johannesburg live in areas that have lower murder rates than the average person in St Louis, Missouri. In eThekwini, with its higher overall murder rate and much less concentration, about 50 per cent of the people in the city live in areas with murder rates below that in St Louis. In Cape Town, it's about 40 per cent. More than a tenth of those in each of the three cities live in areas with murder rates lower than the average in Washington, DC.

The safest parts of South Africa are as safe as anywhere in the world. There just aren't very many of them and very few people live in them. Large areas of South African cities have rates of violence that are definitely very high by the standards of most cities in the developed world, but not all of them and not exceptionally so. So there are fewer parts of Chicago with murder rates above 35 per 100 000 than there are in Cape Town, and more parts with rates below 5.[53] Then there are a handful of places in South Africa with rates of violence matched only by the very worst in Central and Latin America. These neighbourhoods are often highly populous. Most of South Africa's relatively well-off are not as safe from fatal violence as the well-off in safer parts of the world, but they are not at anywhere near the risk suggested by the national or city average murder rates. On the other hand, South Africa's least well-off face risks about as bad as it gets anywhere, at many times the national rate. Although just kilometres apart, they may as well live in different worlds.

Smaller concentration

Even a single precinct is quite a large and often diverse area, including more than one suburb, many thousands or tens of thousands of people, plus roads, businesses, houses of different levels of formality, flats, schools, parks, undeveloped land, and so on. A lot of research over the last 30 years has shown that crime is often very narrowly concentrated. Within each precinct, some crimes may be fairly evenly distributed, but others likely centre on just one or a handful of hotspots, each the size of perhaps a block or a segment of a street. One famous study found that half of all the calls to the police in a crime-ridden American city came from less than 3 per cent of street addresses.[54] The reason for the concentration depends on the nature and generators of each crime. For example, thefts from motor vehicles in Gauteng often concentrate around shopping centres.[55] So even to speak of a precinct's recorded figures as representing to its inhabitants a given risk of crime may not make much sense, as the risk faced by someone currently in one small section of the precinct may be many times greater than the risk faced by that same person when they move just a block or two away.

Many crimes may also show temporal concentrations – occurring far more often at a certain time of year, month, week or day. For example, a lot of violent crime in South Africa is associated with the use of alcohol and other drugs, so rates of especially interpersonal violence tend to rise at times and in places where there is more alcohol and drug consumption.

Weekends, especially long weekends, and holidays are therefore associated with more violent crime. Mortuary figures
suggest that violent deaths in South Africa peak in December
through the year, and on Saturdays and Sundays through the
week.[56] Some research has also found that violent crimes in
various countries tend to peak in summer, whereas property
crimes peak in winter.[57] The much-criticised fact that the SAPS
releases its figures only on a yearly basis confounds regular
analysis to untangle these patterns in time, but what they mean
is that even within one small section of one precinct, the level
of risk faced by someone at one point in time may be many
times greater than for that some person in that same spot a few
hours, days or months later.

The SAPS Crime Administration System routinely captures
some level of time and geographic detail for recorded crimes.[58]
Each station should have the capacity to map its reported crimes
in space and time on an ongoing basis, and a dedicated crime
information officer should compile crime threat and crime
pattern analyses in order to brief other officers. According to
the SAPS, over 56 000 station and cluster crime threat analysis
reports were compiled in 2014/2015.[59] These analyses and the
data on which they are based are not usually made public,
but should ideally feed constantly into operational planning.
Unfortunately, there is evidence that at least some of the
highest-crime stations do not appear to have a functioning
system to produce these reports.[60]

But even were it possible to narrow in on the risk of a given crime to the 'average person' at a certain time of day and year, and in a certain small section of a precinct, we would still be missing some of the biggest factors that determine the relative risks of crime victimisation. Age and gender differences are vast. In 2014/2015, adult men were the victims in 83 per cent of the recorded murders, 66 per cent of the serious assaults and 14 per cent of the sexual offences.[61] While women are disproportionately affected by sexual crimes and assault that happens in the home, men are disproportionately likely to be victims of most recorded interpersonal crimes.[62] Some of this disparity may be due to reporting dynamics that are difficult to quantify, for example because women are much more likely than men to be assaulted by an intimate partner than by a stranger or someone else in their community, which can affect reporting both to the police and in surveys. South Africa's murder rate among women is very high (about five times the global rate),[63] but the bulk of the people murdered in South Africa (and most of the world) are men, and the bulk of those men are under the age of 34.[64] If we disaggregate the mortuary-based murder rate by gender, we therefore find that the rate for men is about 67 per 100 000, while that for women is about 11.[65] Elderly people of both genders are also less likely than their younger counterparts to be victims of most crimes. For a range of reasons, people of different ages and genders interact with their spaces and peers in very different ways, making for very different crime victimisation profiles even within the same or closely adjacent spaces. Research and analysis on crime needs to disaggregate by these factors wherever possible, but the official figures are often a poor data source for these purposes. Despite living in the same household, two people will for reasons related to gender and age (and a range of other characteristics) experience different worlds of crime.

• • •

The national crime figures are a tempting barometer of crime and safety, and in a very limited sense they can fulfil this role. They do so at the cost of grossly oversimplifying what is happening in the lives of the people in the country. Crime is quite different from one province to another; from the major metros to the areas beyond them; from one city to another; from one precinct to another nearby; from someone of a given age, gender and population group (and also disability status, sexuality and a host of other factors we haven't explored here) to someone occupying a different social space. And this is to say nothing of the disparate impact and significance that the same legally defined crime may have in different lives. A given financial loss can irritate one person and devastate another. An assault can be shrugged off by one but cause another to make lasting changes in how they interact with their world. These differences may not be easily discerned by those in different social positions. Knowledge based on our own experiences or those filtered through to us through informal networks or the press are the kinds that probably resonate most for many people, but the usual problem of generalisability from such data is arguably exaggerated in the case of South Africa, which has always been and remains so deeply socially and spatially divided. Whereas the national rates of crime are an interesting abstraction, their highly localised detail is the tangible experience. A walk or short drive can transport you between entirely different worlds of crime. So can a few years of passing time.

So far we have explored some of what can be gleaned by comparing the national crime statistics to those of other countries and by slicing them more finely to show how they vary within the country. The crucial thing we have missed is that none of what we have described is fixed. Should we take a similar snapshot in a decade's time, it would look different. The levels and concentrations of crime are subject to a degree of inertia,[66] such that last year's crime rate is usually a strong predictor of this year's, but they are far from rigid.[67] Crime conditions are constantly changing. The countries, cities or neighbourhoods with the lead now in whatever crime may only recently have taken it. For example, Cape Town only took its clear murder lead in the last couple of years, as we'll discuss in the final chapter. The past can be a very foreign country. Each of over 1 000 precincts in the country has seen a different and shifting mix of the recorded levels of each of dozens of crimes over the years, and although we don't have such data on that level, each has also seen its own trends in terms of reporting rates. This massively complicated patchwork is inevitably smoothed into near meaninglessness as it is aggregated to the national level. We encourage you to peruse the official statistics release or one of the more user-friendly platforms for yourself,[68] to see exactly how many of what crimes have been recorded in the areas where you live, work or play in each of the last ten years. Unless you're fairly involved with your police station or other local safety structures, or you regularly take representative polls, it may well surprise you. People's perceptions of what is happening with crime are often entirely at odds with not only the official rates but also self-reported rates of victimisation.[69]

Although this book can't tell you the crime risks and how they have changed in the areas that matter to you, it can give an overview of some important features of the macro context that may help with interpreting the micro. In the next chapter, we describe as well as possible what the murder statistics of over a century can tell us about crime and social structures in South Africa in the long term. This should help us get closer to an understanding of our present and future.

5

A national history of murder, 1911–2015

As we have discussed, historical crime figures in South Africa become more sketchy and unreliable with every year further back in time. Differences in policing reach, capacity and approach proliferate. In the first half of the twentieth century, the South African Police (SAP) was an entirely different institution, or rather cluster of institutions, to what it is today. It began trying to standardise its criminal statistics collection process from 1921,[1] but it was wracked by internal politics and stretched thin by a series of strikes, riots and two world wars, and in any event it only assumed full responsibility for the whole Union in 1936. Nevertheless, with a few small gaps where the figures aren't available, Figure 7 represents the raw official figures for the number of murders (or, more properly, alleged or suspected murders) as recorded and released by the SAP until 1993.

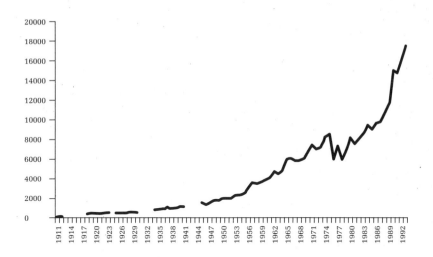

Figure 7: Official SAP recorded murder figures, 1911–1993

The number of murders reported in 1993 was more than 400 times larger than that in 1911 and about eight times larger than that in 1950. The figures rose fairly steadily until the mid-1970s, then dropped and fluctuated considerably (likely due at least in part to shifts in the official borders, as we'll show below), before rising again in the early 1980s and at a very rapid rate in the second half of that decade. Changes in the definitions and manner of presenting the figures for other crimes make it difficult to compare their trends over a longer period, but the trend in official figures for other violent crimes is broadly similar. For example, between 1986 and 1993, while the number of murders went up by 80 per cent, the number of robberies with aggravating circumstances went up by 123 per cent, the number of reported rapes went up 71 per cent, and the number of serious assaults went up 32 per cent.

125

Such figures are useful in giving a sense of the demands made on such institutions as the police and mortuaries. Even leaving aside the matter of unrecorded crimes, however, they do not themselves provide a very useful impression of how large the average person's risk was of being murdered. There were of course far more people in the country in 1993 than there were in 1911. We need to turn the murder figures into rates.

Population estimates prior to 1994 were erratic and of poor quality, and it isn't always clear what parts of the country the SAP considered its official jurisdiction – never mind where it had meaningful coverage. The SAP provides its estimated national population figure in annual reports until 1976, at which point it is just over 27 million. It then fails to give updated estimates or any hints for a good few years, but we can extrapolate from rates that its population estimate in 1987 was 17.5 million. So in about a decade in which the real national population probably grew by about 8 million,[2] the SAP has instead managed to lose almost 10 million people. We do know from the annual reports that Transkei's crime figures are excluded from the reported totals as of 1976. It is likely that this accounts for the year's sudden drop, quite unlike the pattern to that point. Another such dip is seen in 1978, and it may well be at this point that the crime figures for Bophuthatswana and possibly Venda are also excluded. We know that by 1987, the SAP was using a population estimate that corresponded to the number living in so-called white areas only – i.e. excluding both the 'independent homelands' (Transkei, Bophuthatswana, Venda

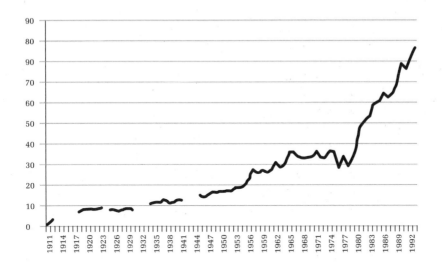

Figure 8: Estimated recorded murder rate per 100 000 within the SAP jurisdiction

and Ciskei) and the 'non-independent homelands' (Gazankulu, Lebowa, QwaQwa, KaNgwane, KwaNdebele and KwaZulu). Records in these parts of the country were extremely poor or nonexistent, so that we simply do not have a numerical account of the crime experienced by the many millions that lived there.

Assuming that the major dips in the official SAP murder figures correspond to jurisdictional cuts, we can piece together population estimates from the SAP, the Central Statistical Service and the South African Institute of Race Relations (SAIRR). This makes it possible to get a rough impression of what the recorded risk of murder was for those people within the SAP jurisdiction (see Figure 8).

This pattern is not so very different from that in the raw

murder figures, but crucially it now has some comparative value. By this reckoning, South Africa has had an official murder rate well above the current global average since at least the 1920s. If, as we've said, murder rates internationally are now considered high when above 20 per 100 000, and very high when above 30,[3] South Africa has been a high-murder-rate country since the 1950s, and a very high one since the 1960s. In the 1980s, it took off extraordinarily, to reach levels of fatal violence almost or entirely without peer at the time.

Lest this all seem methodological or mathematical trickery, note that we know from other sources that criminal gangs have terrorised miners and township residents for over a century;[4] that the early South African Police were already in the mid-1920s lamenting the very high rates of serious crime as compared, for example, to Australia;[5] that there were grave concerns about rising levels of juvenile delinquency in Johannesburg from the mid-1930s;[6] and that from the 1950s crime and violence played a major destabilising role in the lives of urban Africans.[7] In 1957 it was already noted that there had been an 'almost steady increase in delinquency and crime over the last several decades', although, at least for white South Africans, the situation was as yet such that 'relatively little attention has been paid to the problem of crime and delinquency' in the country.[8] But by the late 1970s the local press acknowledged our crime rate as 'one of the highest in the world',[9] and as 'among the most violently escalating in the world'.[10] By the early 1980s, the murder rate was ranked as the second highest in the world.[11] In the late

1980s, violent crime was described as 'rocketing'.[12] Using different population estimates, other sources calculated murder rates even higher than those indicated here, to the 80s and even 90s per 100 000 by 1993.[13]

All of this must be seen in the context that official crime figures excluded the 'independent and self-governing states', that very little police time was devoted to crime, and that reporting rates for other serious crimes in the most affected areas were as low as 27 per cent.[14] It can hardly be emphasised enough that the official figures are without doubt a large undercount of the number of people who lost their lives to murder within our borders then or now.

Still, the official statistics can help reveal something we might otherwise have missed and make it possible not just to draw an interesting line on a graph, but also to help make sense of when and how things came to be as they are now. In our view, there are four clear phases in the old South Africa's murder rate that can be associated in turn with modernisation, dislocation, repression and manipulation, and political disintegration. First, in the phase of modernisation, the murder rate shows a steady increase to the 1950s. This corresponds with a period of major urbanisation and industrialisation. Gold mining and manufacturing expanded rapidly, and with them the size and number of townships or 'locations'. The total urban population more than quadrupled in size in 40 years.[15] This meant the radical reorganisation of structures of authority, gender, family, space and values for countless South Africans.[16]

As we saw in the chapter on international comparison, these processes are strongly associated with rising crime rates.

The phase of dislocation saw South African murder rates increase rapidly from the mid-1950s to stabilise at very high levels by the mid-1960s. The National Party came to power in 1948 and the Population Registration Act and Group Areas Act were passed in 1950, and within a few years began the large-scale forcible removal of millions of people from their homes. Within the next two decades, countless communities, social networks and ways of living were utterly destroyed. Further, the trauma had to be endured in conditions of chronic over-crowding, exclusion, insecurity and ongoing indignity. The murder rate more than doubled in 15 years, and by the mid-1960s it would have placed us within today's list of the top ten most violent places in the world.

The period 1965–1980, associated with repression and manipulation, was exceptional in that it did not see a con-sistent increase in the official murder rate. The reasons for this are probably at least twofold. Apartheid was at its height and justifying itself as the prevention of crime and disorder, with huge investments in the policing of boundaries and the exclusion of those considered inherently dangerous from the areas deemed worthy of defence and protection.[17] Briefly, widespread repression was relatively effective at shoring itself up. Crime-combating resources were highly concentrated in the areas with relatively little crime, while those with crime levels by now already very high saw little ordinary policing.[18]

The stability in the murder rate in this period is due also to more explicit jurisdictional manipulation, with policing for a large proportion of the population officially delegated to the Bantustan authorities.

The 1980s brought a new phase, that of political disintegration, with the already very high murder rate spiralling wildly upwards. Some of this can be ascribed to the intensification of the struggle against apartheid, to political conflict and to attempts to make the townships ungovernable. But the distinction between 'ordinary' criminal activities and those in some direct way associated with politics is a difficult one, not least as while on the one hand the state sought to strip township activists of legitimacy by labelling them criminals and terrorists, on the other hand some 'comrades' did commit criminal acts in the name of politics.[19] Politics were criminalised, and criminality was politicised. A single event could be at once a political protest and a riot involving gratuitous violence and looting.[20] As such, it can never be clear what proportion of the murders around this period were related to political conflict. Estimates at the time from the SAIRR, derived from a number of sources and monitoring agencies, saw political fatalities rise from about 10 per cent of murder figures in the mid-1980s to a fifth or at most a quarter in the early 1990s.[21] The SAP estimated that political motives accounted for about 20 per cent of the murders in 1993.[22] We also know that recorded rates of other crimes – including robbery, assault and rape – rose considerably during this period.

Although of course politics may play complex roles in their causes, these crimes are arguably less directly attributable to sincere political goals. Comparative research has shown that periods of political upheaval also raise the rates of crimes not related to politics, as state legitimacy, capacity and social structures become more unstable.[23] So the 1980s saw escalating chaos and violence, as well as declining capacity on the part of the state to police its boundaries. The murder rate rise was dramatic and it seemed inexorable.

After transition

As of 1994, we have figures that officially include the crimes recorded against the roughly 7 million people in the 'independent homelands' and 9.5 million in the 'non-independent homelands'. This makes for a sharp spike of more than half in the murder figures, from about 17 000 in 1993 to about 27 000 in 1994. From this we can work out that the recorded murder rate in the former 'homelands' was also extremely high, at about 58 per 100 000 people. This probably represents a large undercount, as policing, reporting and record-keeping could by no means become functional overnight. More likely, a number of the social, political and institutional factors that compromised the accuracy of the older statistics might have been expected to improve gradually over the years that followed. Predictions of what crime rates would do following transition varied wildly, according to different estimates of the relative significance of

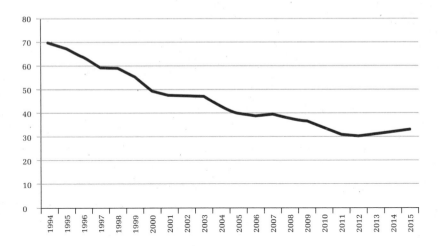

Figure 9: SAPS recorded murder rate per 100 000 from 1994 to 2015

such factors as underreporting, political legitimacy, styles of policing and social instability.[24]

With the settling of national borders and the improvement of census data, population estimates have become easier to work with (with the relatively minor exception of updating population estimates around census years, as discussed earlier), so as of 1994 we can more comfortably rely on rates per 100 000 to make the figures comparable. The annual official recorded murder rate from 1994 to 2015, as released by the SAPS, is shown in Figure 9.

Astonishingly and almost overnight, a rapid escalation in violence was halted and began a steady reversal. The national murder rate has more than halved, meaning that the average person in the country is less than half as likely to be murdered today as they were 20 years ago. At around 30 per 100 000, the murder rate is now at a level it hasn't been since the 1970s (although note that the raw figures are of course much higher, meaning that the absolute case load they represent for the police or mortuaries is double what it was then). On the best official numerical account that we have, this country has never been as violent as it was in 1993–1994. In 1994, the SAPS recorded almost 27 000 murders in the country, or about 74 a day. Last year, it recorded less than 18 000, or about 49 a day, and this in a population that has grown since then by about 40 per cent. A decline of that magnitude and speed is best described as a plummet. It is in line with the rate of decline in crime rates in New York City, around which so many theories have been spun.

We have shown that we have no reason to believe that any more than a small proportion of the dead bodies apparently due to unnatural causes are failing to make it into the police figures. This proportion also seems to have fallen, with for example about 15 per cent of people not reporting murders to the police in 1998 as compared to less than 5 per cent in 2015.[25] Other data sources corroborate the trend, and also suggest that it underestimates the decline, as the undercount has progressively shrunk. In 1998, one in 200 households surveyed said they had experienced an incident of murder in the last year.[26] In 2003, it was one in 500.[27] In 2015, it was one in 1 000.[28] People also report being much less afraid of murder than they used to be. It has dropped steadily down the rankings for the crimes most feared and those considered most common. Further, although for reasons we've discussed they do not match very closely, both vital registration and mortuary data have corroborated the trend.[29] South Africa is still a very violent country by global standards, but there is every reason to believe that it is far less so than it was 20 years ago. How is it that this huge reduction in fatal violence over the last two decades isn't something we rejoice over, talk about or even seem to be aware of as a nation? This is one of the most dramatic and unequivocal features in the history of South African crime, and no one seems to have paid it much attention.

There are a number of reasons why many might find it hard to believe. As political conflict abated from the mid-1990s, masses of media and public attention were freed up and finally started catching up with the issue of crime.[30] Stories of violence are highly memorable, and our minds tend to generalise from that which is easy to recall. So we tend to think 'newsworthy' events are far more common than they are, and more common even than more mundane ones. Stories of violent death also reach and interest more people than stories of people living their lives through to old age – thus the media cliché, 'If it bleeds, it leads.'[31] As Steven Pinker puts it in his account of the decline in violence in the recorded history of large parts of the world, 'No matter how small the percentage of violent deaths may be, in absolute terms there will always be enough of them to fill the evening news, so people's impressions of violence will be disconnected from the actual proportions.'[32] In the South African case, the absolute numbers remain very high, so this is doubly true.

Another factor is that as long as people are still dying horribly, having traumatic experiences of other crimes and living with daily fear, it can seem absurd and insensitive to suggest that there is any good news worth telling. Every murder is a tragedy. As critical as it is for the broader society, it makes little difference to the deceased or to those affected that a given murder is one of a smaller number than last year. The suggestion that the country is safer now than ever before in most people's memory leads not just to incredulity, but often to anger. One might be accused of being part of the 'substantial denialist lobby', set for whatever reason against acknowledging the crisis of crime.[33] Good news seldom goes over well, even in places where there isn't nearly so fraught an association between perceptions of safety and assessments of the national project. Yet people's beliefs about the prevalence of crime, and the strength of the associated fear, have a very poor and sometimes even inverse relationship with their risk of victimisation and their direct experiences of it.[34] This isn't to say that those perceptions and fears are necessarily irrational or wrong – only that they are a very poor measure of how much crime is happening. There are a great many factors that shape our perceptions of crime and that have nothing to do with how much of it we or those around us experience.

To be fair, not every crime type has declined in the last 20 years in the same way as has murder. It may also be that this period has seen significant changes in the distribution of crime and violence, such that some people are indeed at greater risk

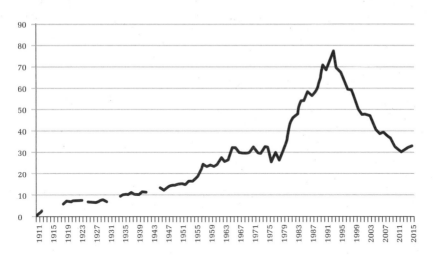

Figure 10: The recorded murder rate over a century

than before, even as others are far safer. As we saw in the last chapter, different people experience levels of risk far higher and others far lower than that suggested by the national murder rate, based on such factors as age, gender, location, race, income level, and so on. These changes in the character of violence, even as the extent of violence is shrinking, may also account for the fact that fear and the perception of violence have not declined in concert with the figures. We will explore some of these dynamics in the next chapter.

For now, let us consider just the national total. Combining everything before the 1994 transition with everything after, the best guess we have for the police's recorded national murder rate in a little over a century of South African history is shown in Figure 10.

In this view, there are three important features to note again,

137

and a fourth to introduce. First, despite an almost certainly large undercount, the South African murder rate has been high by global standards since the 1950s, and very high since the 1960s. Any proposed explanations or solutions for our levels of violence will need to take this into account. If they revolve only around developments since then, they are unlikely to get very far. The second feature is that there is a sharp peak in violence through the 1980s and to 1993. Theories or strategies that fail to take account of that will be markedly incomplete. Third, there was a huge (and we have no reason to believe not 'real') decline between 1994 and 2012. The transition did not fail to reduce levels of national violence. Far less did it mark the beginning of it. On the contrary, it immediately and for almost two decades successfully reversed what had previously seemed a relentless escalation. The 18 years after 1994 represent sustained, cumulative, unprecedented progress in the improvement of the safety of the average person in this country. The extraordinary violence around the transition appears to have abated, arguably returning to the level – still very high – that more accurately reflects underlying structural conditions. This is something we might have missed entirely had we stopped at comparing the murder rate to other countries at one point in time. By taking a longitudinal view of the crime statistics and combining it with other contextual knowledge and theory, we have been able to gain more insight into the likely nature and timing of the key drivers of national levels of violence.

We come, then, to the fourth and final important feature of

this pattern: the noticeable rise since 2012. This is the first such reversal the new South Africa has seen. It may or may not be a matter of particular concern. If the trend soon reverses, it may yet turn out to be a blip, insignificant in the context of the greater decline. A return to the previous downward trajectory, which was an average reduction of 4 per cent a year, could see the murder rate dip below 20 per 100 000 in a little over a decade. That would take us out of the 'high murder' category for the first time in at least three-quarters of a century (although that level of violence would still be nowhere near as low as that enjoyed by most of the developed world). If the trend does not soon reverse, and we are instead seeing the beginning of a significant new upswing in violence, it may be time to begin developing new theories and strategies. These may have to be quite unlike the ones we have relied on in the past. Luckily, we can do a little better than just guess. The crime statistics and other data contain a great deal more information than just what proportion of the people in the country overall have been murdered in the last year. In the next chapter, we take a look at what else we know about how violence has changed in the last 20 years.

6

The changing character of violence, 1994–2015

We've seen that in terms of the recorded national level of fatal violence, South Africa today is a very different place to what it was in 1994 and also a slightly different one to what it was in 2012. There are any number of ways we might go about making sense of this. In this chapter, we speculate, based only on what we might learn from the existing official numbers, from the police investigation dockets and victimisation surveys, about the changing contexts of violence – who kills who and why.

Murder is not, of course, the only crime recorded by the police. In fact, it is one of the rarest. It is sometimes envisioned as the tiny apex of the pyramid of physical violence, with each successive level below it comprising a larger number of less serious incidents.[1] The problem is that the recorded rates of other crimes are far less reliable. The further back in time one goes, the less comparable their statistics are likely to be. There have been numerous changes in legal definitions, in crime categorisation or in the level of disaggregation in the statistics release. Still, it is our view that one of the most powerful ways to bring nuance and value to the crime statistics is to move as far as possible beyond the fixation with year-on-year changes in the numbers. Tracking short-term trends is vital for smaller jurisdictions in order to zero in on changes in specific crime problems, but to the extent that the national scale is appropriate to forming explanations and strategies, the short term is more likely to distort than reveal much that is of use. This book therefore takes the longest view possible for each crime type. Broad trends in rates per 100 000 (or, in a few cases where more appropriate, raw figures) are indicated as of 1994 or the earliest date thereafter for which comparable data exists. For brevity, we refer to the end dates of the relevant reporting year – i.e. when referring to the statistics for crimes registered between 1 April 2014 and 31 March 2015, we will simply say 2015.

It should by now be a familiar refrain that a major problem with tracking and interpreting crime rates over time is that there may have been large changes in the extent to which people report them to the police. In the context especially of changes in policing regimes and social structures, the waterline on the iceberg of crime may rise or fall (i.e. with different propor-tions of it becoming visible in the official figures), confounding assessment of changes in its size or shape. In making sense of, and to some extent corroborating, broad trends, however, victimisation survey data is an invaluable companion to the official police figures. This chapter again demonstrates why this is important.

Because the docket data is poor and out of date, and because there remain major limitations to both the recorded rates of crimes other than murder and the results of victimisation surveys, our conclusions must necessarily be speculative. The most important feature we think can be drawn from the data is that violence has become increasingly instrumental rather than expressive (we will define these terms shortly), meaning that it is now more associated with crimes like robbery than with what the police have termed 'social fabric' crimes. Another interesting point is that there may have been a significant 'democracy reporting bulge' in the period after 1994, but that this progress seems to have been lost subsequently. For a while, people became more likely to report crimes to the police, but then they seemed to have changed their minds. Third, it seems that a larger proportion of robbery is targeting non-strangers than in the past, at least in the Western Cape. This is a distinct phenomenon from other violent crimes, and it is a worrying sign for social relations that may best be explained in the context of gang activities.

A shift in the nature of murder?

Although statistics lump them together, every murder is not the same. Each is the outcome of some kind of conflict between at

least two people, but the circumstances of that conflict, its location, the extent of its premeditation or intention, the weapons
that make it fatal, the intoxicating substances or other factors that may inflame it, and the characteristics of the people
involved can vary and combine in many ways. Two of the most
common means of categorising murder (or aggression or crime
in general) are by the nature or closeness of the relationship
between the perpetrator and the victim and by the motive. Each
may be described at various levels of specificity, but at their
simplest can be placed on a spectrum between stranger and
non-stranger (sometimes called 'primary' and 'non-primary')[2]
relationships and between motives that are either expressive or
instrumental. Expressive motives involve emotional responses
to individuals or situations (such as anger, jealousy or revenge),
whereas instrumental motives are directed at a goal of financial
or other reward. Both may benefit the aggressor, but, whereas
expressive aggression is more reactive and an end in itself,
instrumental aggression is more strategic and rather a means
to some other end.

Of course there may be an overlap between these, but for the
purposes of this explanation the two broad distinctions are
important. There may be crucial differences within these relationship categories or difficulties untangling precise motives.
Murders of employers, of friends, of children and of intimate
partners may well have quite distinct dynamics, although none
of the people involved are strangers. There may be considerable overlap between motives targeted at property and those

arising from some strong spontaneous reaction in the situation. For example, many people seem to believe that South African violence is distinctive in that it is so gratuitous – that more violence is employed than instrumental goals would require or even understandable emotion make sense of.[3] There is also ongoing debate and negotiation about whether violence used in protest should be understood as expressive or instrumental. It may not even be easy always to draw a clear distinction between victim and perpetrator. Moreover, research elsewhere and in South Africa has shown that violent perpetrators tend to be generalists, with patterns of a range of forms of violence against both strangers and non-strangers.[4] In violence against strangers, perpetrators may themselves also make quite poor distinctions between instrumental and expressive motives.[5] Retaliatory or reputational violence may also fit poorly into the dichotomy of expressive or instrumental.

Still, it can be useful to broadly differentiate between whether the people involved in an incident of murder or other crime knew each other and what the main reason was for the crime. Crimes involving different relationships and motives may follow different causal processes, concentrate in different places and need different prevention strategies. Failure to make any distinction between these may mean that we lose such insights as that the peaks in violence common on public holidays are due to expressive violence, whereas in fact instrumental violence may dip at these times.[6] Neighbourhood features do seem to influence patterns in the relationships and motives around murder in different ways, but disadvantaged communities tend to experience heightened levels of both expressive and instrumental violence.[7]

To a large extent, the motive and relationship distinctions tend to overlap. Generally, the closer the relationship between the people, the more likely the motive is to be expressive.[8] It is posited that this is because the level of intimacy works to protect individuals from certain kinds of violence.[9] The better people know each other, the less likely they are to feel justified in instrumental violence; the less well people know each other, the less likely they are to arouse murderously strong emotion. When this isn't the pattern, when significant numbers of non-strangers are targeted for instrumental violence or strangers for expressive violence, these crimes are called non-normative or deviant, as they reflect that the bonds of familiarity are failing to inhibit instrumental crimes and that absence of familiarity is failing to preclude strong emotional reaction.[10] Non-normative murders are thought to require some additional explanation.[11] This is why cases of people killing their spouses with strategic ends in mind are considered far more shocking and newsworthy than the far more numerous cases that occur in fits of rage or jealousy, and why road rage appears so often in the newspapers when street robbery does not. Expressive violence against strangers or instrumental violence against intimates seems wrong. Neighbourhood or cultural factors can raise the proportion of non-normative violence, for example when there is a strong perceived need to protect a reputation for toughness, because known criminal rivals are targeted for robbery, or because the sense of impunity is such that the risk of being identified by victims fails to dissuade predation.[12]

Modern society has tended to take the view that violent behaviour between individuals who have an existing relationship is relatively forgivable, a somewhat unavoidable by-product of that relationship, whereas that between strangers is the random act of a predator who threatens society at large.[13] Although most violent crimes are committed by non-strangers, it is the perceived threat of violence at the hands of a stranger that inspires the greatest fear and grabs the most public attention. This has clear implications for gender justice, as women are disproportionately victimised by intimates. In South Africa, these assumptions also take on a racial character. 'Black-on-black' violence is often implicitly portrayed in the media and the white imagination as something cultural, unavoidable and happening 'somewhere out there', whereas violence experienced by whites is thought to be largely instrumental (but sometimes also non-normative and frightening in its expressive character).[14] Popular thinking in South Africa has tended to assume that relationship type and motivation are largely analogous, that there are two main types of violence: that which is between non-strangers and expressive, and that which is between strangers and instrumental.

The difficulty with this kind of analysis is that it requires considerably better data than just the number of murders that have been brought to police attention. The best place to start

146

should be the murder docket. So far, all we have extracted from these critical documents is the numbers they add up to, but they should also contain a wealth of other information, including some understanding of the nature of the crime, its location and time, the weapons used and injuries sustained, the progress and results of the investigation, the statements from the parties interviewed, and possible linkages with other crimes.[15] There should be capacity for docket analysis at both the station level and the national level.[16] The problem is that if the investigation doesn't get very far, the docket will not have much of use to offer.[17]

One study of dockets in high murder areas found that only about half contained any usable information about the relationship between the victim and the perpetrator or about the circumstances or motive surrounding the murder.[18] This means that, in South Africa, we know little or nothing about the majority of murders that happen.[19] Besides the limitation that the data reflects only what is known to the police, a chronic problem is posed by lost, incomplete or illegible dockets.[20] This makes it very difficult to make sense of what is happening. Still, we should try to determine what the dockets do say.

A sample of murder dockets in Soweto for 1991 and 1992 showed that in just under half of the cases where the relationship between the victim and perpetrator could be established, the two were relatives or knew each other closely.[21] In the late 1990s, the SAPS completed and released the results of a national murder docket analysis. It conflated the relationship and motive distinctions to report that the proportion of what it called 'social murders' was about 80 per cent.[22] These, it said, occurred between people who knew each other, who got into an argument (often drug- or alcohol-fuelled) about the stuff of daily life (money, infidelity, family), which developed into a physical fight and ended up in murder. This profile may well be skewed by the fact that such incidents will make for relatively easy investigations and quicker establishment of motives. However, this general picture of violence in the country was confirmed in other sources, such as victimisation surveys and mortuary data. The vast majority of violence, including murder but also sexual and other assault, occurred between people who knew each other by name or by sight, and of whom either or both were intoxicated.[23] Most violence happened in private homes or places of entertainment. The absence of clear intention to kill meant that about half of the murder and attempted murder cases opened in 2000 that made it to a court verdict were downgraded to charges of culpable homicide or serious assault.[24] It was said that what this showed was that there was a strong pattern of interpersonal conflict resolution through violence.[25] This appears to have been the typical context of South African violence in the late 1990s: between non-strangers and for largely expressive motives.

To a large extent, it probably still is. The most recent national docket analysis released by the SAPS covered a representative sample of murder dockets in 2007/2008. It found that for those murders in which the docket could provide some indication as to the motives and circumstances, about 65 per cent could be categorised as resulting from 'social behaviour'.[26] About half of all the murders reviewed were considered to be the result of an argument or misunderstanding. There was also, however, a different and newly prominent factor: about 16 per cent of the murders reviewed nationally were considered to have been the consequence of another crime, chiefly aggravated robbery. There were other small contributors, such as 5 per cent due to vigilantism, 1.2 per cent due to gang activities and 0.4 per cent due to xenophobia-related incidents, none of which fall very clearly into a dichotomy of expressive or instrumental violence. But deadly violence in the course of another crime (i.e. instrumental violence) was now in a solid if still distant second place to interpersonal conflict (i.e. expressive violence).

Again it is important to note that the detection rate for murder (which reflects the proportion of charges referred to court after identification of a chargeable suspect, withdrawn or closed as unfounded),[27] in 2007/2008 was 28 per cent.[28] We do not know what proportion of murder dockets do not contain enough information even to make a good guess as to motive or circumstances. But based on those dockets where there was some indication, it seems that in the decade to 2008 the proportion of 'social murders' declined from an overwhelming majority to a moderate one, and the proportion of murders that relate to other crimes has grown. An analysis of murder in the Khayelitsha area found that, in 2012, the proportion of 'social murders' could be closer to half.[29] The SAPS has not released results of a national docket analysis since 2009, so we don't know what may have changed since then. Moreover, for reasons we've already explained, victimisation surveys aren't very useful for finding out about murder. What we may be able to do, however, is draw some inferences from the trends in the rates of some other crimes more easily categorised, as long as we place these within the context of what we know about their reporting dynamics.

Trends in assault

Assault is generally an expressive crime and usually happens between people who know each other. Docket analysis has suggested that more than two-thirds of what the police call 'contact crime' or 'crimes against the person' – and most people would call 'violent crime' – occur between people who know each other, either within the family or inner circle of relationships, or within the intermediate circle of acquaintances.[30] Some of these crimes in particular are often, as mentioned above, conceptually clustered in South Africa under the term 'social fabric crime' or 'social crime'.[31] Besides murder, these are attempted murder, assault with the intent to cause grievous bodily harm, common assault and rape. The relationships suggested by the dockets are confirmed in victimisation surveys. In 1998, 60 per cent of assault victims and 63 per cent of sexual offence victims said that they knew the perpetrator by name, and a further 17 per cent of assault and 12 per cent of sexual offence victims knew the perpetrator by sight.[32]

'Common' assault involves the 'unlawful and intentional (a) direct or indirect application of force to the body of another person, or (b) threat of application of immediate personal violence to another, in circumstances in which the threatened person is prevailed upon to believe that the person who is threatening him or her has the intention and power to carry out his threat'.[33] Assault with the intent to cause grievous bodily harm, usually called assault GBH, involves 'the unlawful and intentional direct or indirect application of force to the body of another person with the intention of causing grievous bodily harm to that person'.[34] Most often the feature that turns a common assault into an assault GBH is the use of a weapon. The line between attempted murder and especially assault GBH may not always be immediately clear, as it mostly comes down to intention. This group of crimes often happen in similar circumstances and tend to have high recorded rates in the same areas.

The police label this cluster as less policeable, as they are poorly preventable with conventional policing tools such as roadblocks and crime intelligence, although victim support and bringing perpetrators to justice may conceivably help with deterrence. Besides murder, we know that few of these crimes have high reporting rates. Still, Figure 11 shows their trends in the official rates. Note that the less serious forms of assault are far more common, so they are scaled to the axis on the left

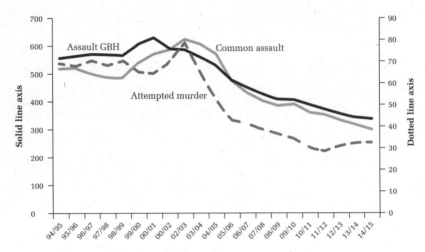

Figure 11: Recorded rates of selected interpersonal crimes

and have solid lines, whereas attempted murder is scaled to the axis on the right and has a dotted line.

Like murder, each of these crimes has a rate in 2015 that is well below what it was in 1995. Attempted murder is down by 53 per cent (the same margin as murder); assault GBH is down 39 per cent; and common assault is down 42 per cent. Since 2012, in which we have seen a slight increase in murder rates, there has also been an increase in attempted murder, but not in the others. Unlike murder, these show a peak somewhere between 2001 and 2003, followed by a strong decline. This requires explanation. Given that docket analysis and logic suggest a close relationship between these crimes and murder, it seems implausible that they should continue rising as murder fell, and only peak seven or eight years later.[35] It may be that reporting dynamics are at play.

Luckily, the series of national victimisation surveys since 1998 have asked people about whether they have recently experienced an assault and whether they reported it to the police. The apparently large improvement in the average person's safety from physical attack indicated in the official figures is often dismissed due to these crimes' low reporting rates according to victimisation surveys, but this involves a selective reading of those surveys, as they also suggest that the proportion of people who tell the survey staff they have experienced such a crime has in fact fallen far more than the official rates. In 1998, 4.2 per cent of respondents said that they had experienced an assault in the last year, and 38 per cent of those said that they had reported it to the police.[36] In 2003, the self-reported victimisation rate had dropped to 2.2 per cent.[37] This struck the authors as so implausible, especially given the rise in the official figures, that they concluded that what must have happened was that the survey 'captured only the most serious assaults, suggesting that the public has become hardened to the point that minor incidents are no longer reported to fieldworkers'.[38] There may be something to this, as we'll discuss below. On the other hand, of those who said they had experienced an assault, the reporting rate had risen to 55 per cent, which would itself account for a large proportion of the increase in the official rate.[39] In 2007, the victimisation rate was down to 1.3 per cent and the reporting rate up to 76 per cent.[40] By 2011, the victimisation rate had seen little change, but the reporting rate had dropped back down to 49 per cent.[41] Since then, the victimisation rate has fallen further, to just 0.1 per cent

The deficiency of official figures on sexual offences

Although rape and sexual assault are considered to be among the most 'social crimes', note that we have not addressed changes in the recorded rates of rape or other sexual crimes. There are three reasons for this. First, the extent to which official figures reflect their real prevalence is subject to some dispute but is widely believed to be extremely limited. This means that it isn't clear how changes in the official rate of sexual crimes should be interpreted.[42] Their reporting rate as suggested in the national victimisation surveys is too variable to make much sense of (46 per cent in 1998, 94 per cent in 2011, 63 per cent in 2015). Second, non-specialised victimisation surveys are also understood to be a poor indicator of the real prevalence or changes in rates of sexual crimes. Among other things, their household setting (which is not private and may well contain the perpetrator) is not conducive to sharing such sensitive information with a stranger.[43]

Third, the last two decades have seen a number of changes in the laws and recording practices around sexual offences. There was a major legal change in the definitions of various sexual offences in December 2007, for example expanding the definition of rape from only vaginal penetration with a penis to vaginal, anal and oral penetration with any object – meaning, among other things, that rape of men is included from that point. The SAPS has also from year to year reported sexual offences with varying levels of disaggregation. Until 2014 it publicised figures for 'total sexual offences' in the initial release of figures, and then the two largest subcategories, namely, rape and sexual assault, separately in the addendum to the annual report. For the 2015 release, it has also removed sexual crimes detected by police action (which refers mostly to sex work and child pornography-related offences) from the category of total sexual offences, and it has not yet released any figures for rape. All told, there is no even minimally comparable data for sexual offences for longer than a handful of years at a stretch. The official data we consider in this book are an extremely poor source of knowledge about sexual crimes, so we do not attempt to make use of them for this purpose.

in 2015, and the reporting rate seems in the last few years to have stabilised somewhere roughly around 50 per cent.[44]

By respondents' own recollection of their experiences, there has in the last 20 years been a fairly steady reduction in assault, to an extent in fact a good deal larger than is reflected in the official rates. It does not strike us as likely that a hardening of attitudes could possibly account for much of such a dramatic decline in self-reported victimisation of non-fatal assault, especially given the large reduction in the much less equivocal official rate of fatal assault over the same period. And the fact that rates of assault first rose and only later fell are exactly what one would predict under conditions of improving police–community relationships and statistical reach and capacity. The rise in the official rates of assault to about 2003 corresponds exactly with a dramatic rise in reporting rates. This was to varying degrees absorbed by categorisation as attempted murder, assault GBH or common assault. The decline in the rates of assault since about 2003 has to some extent been hastened by a drop in reporting (although not yet nearly to the low levels of 1998), but to a greater extent it almost certainly is due to an ongoing real decline. These lower levels of the interpersonal violence pyramid have shrunk just as has the apex of murder.

There seems to have been a few years of police and communities sizing each other up, a few years of surge in the reporting of physical violence even as its real victimisation rates fell, followed by a continuing decline in assault but now also some decline in reporting. In other words, the rise in the official figures for these crimes to the early 2000s was not the result of an increase in the victimisation rate of these crimes, but instead the result of more of them being reported in what we might call a 'democracy reporting bulge', even as their rates were falling. If reporting dynamics had held stable, the line on the graph would show a more sustained downward trend. Instead, large underreporting suppressed it, then a surge in reporting raised it, then a decline in reporting again pushed it down faster than it was continuing to fall. This can be represented as in Figure 12.

The context of assault

According to victimisation surveys, people assault each other for much the same motives as before – largely anger and jealousy.[45] They also have much the same relationships to each

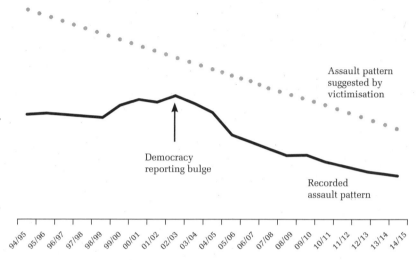

The changing character of violence, 1994–2015

Assault pattern
suggested by
victimisation

Democracy
reporting bulge

Recorded
assault pattern

94/95 95/96 96/97 97/98 98/99 99/00 00/01 01/02 02/03 03/04 04/05 05/06 06/07 07/08 08/09 09/10 10/11 11/12 12/13 13/14 14/15

Figure 12: Suggested relationship between reporting and victimisation for assault

other. In 1998, about 20 per cent of assault victims said that they did not know the perpetrator by name or by sight.[46] The answer options have changed but in 2015, the proportion that said their assault had been at the hands of either an 'unknown community member' or 'unknown people from outside' was about 27 per cent.[47] People who assault each other still know each other and seem to be similarly motivated. We cannot defensibly derive the gender dimension of the context of assault from these sources, especially because such a large proportion of women's assailants are likely to be within the home.

According to what people report in surveys, there does appear to have been some change in the average seriousness of assault. In 1998, about 49 per cent of assault victims said that they had been injured, and 76 per cent of those said that they had required medical attention.[48] In 2003, 73 per cent of assault victims said that they had sustained injuries, 78 per cent of which required medical attention.[49] In 2015, about 80 per cent said they had sustained injuries in their assault, 75 per cent of whom said they had required medical attention.[50] Some of this may have been due to the fact that the assaults that respondents thought worth mentioning were more serious than they had been before. The proportion of assaults that result in some injury seems to have increased, even as the number of assaults has decreased. This may be because assaults have become less casual. Assailants are more likely to really mean it.

It may also be that there has been some change in the lethality of assault. Changes in access to emergency medical care and the availability of firearms can affect what proportion of assaults results in death.[51] This period saw the country's firearm regulation system overhauled by the introduction of the Firearms Control Act (FCA), fully implemented in 2004, which out of concern for their prominent role in violent crime sought to reduce the number of firearms in circulation in the country.[52] Licensing conditions were made stricter, there were amnesties on legal and illegal gun hand-ins to the authorities, and as many as 300 000 weapons were destroyed.[53] Gun advocates take exception to any claims of success around this process, but mortuary data does suggest that the period of implementation of the Act was associated with a more rapid decline in murders involving firearms than murder by other means.[54] Firearms do seem to be responsible for a smaller proportion of deaths now than they were at least 10 years ago.[55] Their control may have helped reduce the lethality of assault. For the most part, however, the main change in assault over the last 20 years seems to be that there is simply much less of it happening.

Trends in robbery

Robbery is generally considered to be the textbook example of stranger violence,[56] as well as instrumental crime in which the offender seeks to maximise gain while minimising risk.[57] It involves violence or threatened violence used as a means to the end of criminally acquiring others' property. It differs from burglary in that it involves the threat or use of force, and it can either be 'common' or it can be 'aggravated' by the use of a weapon or some other circumstance, such as its location. Common robbery may be forceful or violent but does not involve the intent to inflict grievous bodily harm. It usually involves grabbing the item in question, perhaps involving a threat or a tussle – e.g. muggings or 'smash and grabs'. As with assault, robbery can be conceptualised as having a pyramid distribution, with more serious incidents (such as robbery that involves a murder) at the relatively small apex, with each successive level below it comprising a larger number of less serious incidents. Common robbery makes up the base of the robbery pyramid, but is likely reported at much lower rates than more serious robberies, such that the recorded rates may reflect the reverse.[58]

Robbery may, depending especially on its target, be anywhere between entirely opportunistic and highly organised and pre-meditated. As different forms of robbery have become matters of concern, the category of aggravated robbery has come to be further broken down in its reporting over time, so that it now consists of bank robbery, robbery of cash in transit, carjacking, truck hijacking, public or street robbery, robbery at residential premises and robbery at non-residential premises. The major-ity of robberies, however, do not involve banks, armoured cars, vehicles, houses or businesses. Most of them happen in the streets.[59] In 1998, about one in 40 respondents to the national victimisation survey said they had experienced some form of robbery in the last year,[60] and about 40 per cent of those said that they had reported it to the police.[61] The trends in the offi-cial figures since then have been as shown in Figure 13.

These trends are not entirely unlike those we saw for assault. The recorded rates of robbery largely rise to 2003 and then decline, although to a lesser extent, such that they are slightly higher in 2015 than they were in 1995. Aggravated robbery dif-fers from common robbery in that it has seen an increase since 2012.

It is difficult to work out exactly what to make of these trends in the official figures, because the national victimisa-tion surveys haven't made consistent distinctions between the different forms and levels of seriousness of robbery. Their results suggest slight but not dramatic improvement in robbery victimisation rates through the period between 1998 and 2007, and again between 2010 and 2015. However, between those

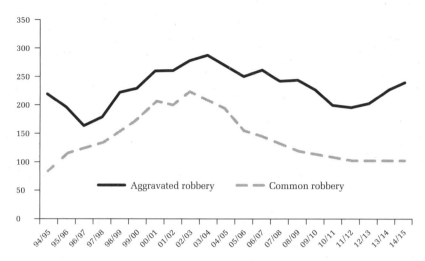

Figure 13: Recorded rates of robbery

dates there was a change in the format of the relevant question (with home robbery and carjacking listed separately), so that it isn't possible to be definitive about the change in self-reported prevalence.[62] Here too there is the possibility that hardening attitudes see a smaller proportion of the incidents remembered and recounted. The lack of consistency in the questions also makes it difficult to make sense of reporting rates. However, it does seem that robbery victimisation rates as a whole have declined slightly in the last two decades. Whereas one in 40 said that they had experienced a robbery of any kind in 1998, in 2007 it was one in 50. In 2010 it was one in 60, excluding home robbery and carjacking, and in the last few years this has dropped further to one in 120. House robbery is less clear.[63]

Between at least 1995 and 2003, there appears to have been a significant relationship between official rates of murder and of robbery, although one declined steadily while the other rose, especially in areas with high rates of both.[64] Specifically, murder rates declined most slowly in the places where robbery increased fastest. Docket analysis in selected high murder areas for the period 2001–2005 has also suggested that robberies accounted for about a quarter of the murders where the circumstances were known, and probably the majority of the large proportion where the circumstances were unknown.[65] To better understand the changing patterns of this form of violence, we must consider the various subcategories of aggravated robbery. The official figures suggest that the declines to 2012 were driven primarily by declines in carjacking and street robbery, whereas since at least 2005 there may have been increases in house and business robbery, and that rates of a number of robbery types have increased since 2012.

Subcategories of aggravated robbery

We begin with the two smallest contributors to the robbery total: bank robberies and robberies of cash in transit. Because they are so rare and variable, they are assessed not as rates per 100 000 in the national population but as raw figures of reports. Since these crimes began to be reported separately, the number of bank robberies in the country has declined by 97 per cent, from a high of just under 500 incidents in 1997 to fewer than 20 in 2015. They fell slowly to about 2001 and then precipitously to 2004, since when they have fluctuated at a relatively low level. Cash-in-transit robberies have taken a more unsteady path, with sometimes a few years of increase and then a few of decrease, but their number has also declined to date by about 70 per cent, from about 400 in 1997 to about 100 in 2015.

These reductions have come in the context of technological development and extensive cooperation between the SAPS and the banking industry and transit companies, for example since about 2001 through the South African Banking Risk Intelligence Centre (SABRIC). Cash-in-transit robberies and bank robberies are considered among the most highly organised crimes.[66] They require a number of relatively highly skilled participants and considerable planning, and a single network may be responsible for a large proportion of these incidents. As a result, they are highly preventable through effective crime intelligence, and may fluctuate considerably as new networks form or are eliminated. ATM bombings may, depending on circumstances, be recorded as any combination of murder or attempted murder, bank or cash-in-transit robbery, malicious damage to property, theft or transgressions of the Explosives Act.[67] Based on records drawn from the banking sector, the period from 2005 saw a marked increase in ATM bombings,[68] but these appear now to have stabilised and somewhat decreased.[69] The cost of these crimes can be considerable and they can certainly involve fatal violence, but they are far too small in number to make a significant contribution to the murder rate.

Next, we can consider the rates of carjacking (or car hijacking) and truck hijacking. The 1990s saw heightened concern in the press about carjacking, so that it began to be disaggregated from robbery in 1997. According to the latest national victimisation survey, about 86 per cent of the people who had experienced a car hijacking had reported it to the police.[70] These reporting rates are higher than for any other crime besides murder, and they have been high for at least the last few years. This is probably because few people can recover from such a large financial shock without insurance, and insurance claims require that you have a case number.[71] On the other hand, it does raise incentives for false reports, with it generally believed that a potentially large proportion of both vehicle and truck hijacking reports are fraudulent.[72]

The pattern in the official figures has gone through a couple of cycles of a few years of increase followed by a few of more dramatic decrease – two steps forward, one step back, in other words. In 2005, the official rates were almost a third lower than their late 1990s peak. After a few more years of growth, there was a rapid drop from 2009 to their lowest point on record, of 18 per 100 000 in 2012. In 2015 carjacking had risen again to 24 per 100 000, but was still about a quarter lower than in 1997. The rates of a number of crimes seem to have dropped around the 2009–2011 period. The police ascribed this to highly visible and intelligence-led policing around the Confederations Cup in 2009 and the World Cup in 2010, but also stressed that this was the beginning of a new era rather than a once-off effort.[73] The subsequent rise suggests this was not quite the case. The downward trend in carjacking over the entire period in the rates suggested in victimisation surveys has been more dramatic. These have declined from one in about 70 in 1998, to one in 250 in 2007, to one in 1 000 in 2015.

Because there are few occurrences and there is little reason that these should vary with population, truck hijacking (like bank robbery and robbery of cash in transit) is more appropriately assessed in terms of real figures rather than rates per 100 000 people. Ideally the figures would be expressed as a proportion of the number of trucks on the road, but such figures are not reliably available. When they began to be disaggregated in 1997, truck hijacking figures were in the midst of an even more dramatic increase than carjacking. There followed a plummet from well over 5 000 incidents in 1999 to about 900 in 2004. In the years since, they rose somewhat to 1 437 in 2009, dipped with many other crimes for the next three years, and have been rising again from 2013. The number of truck hijackings in 2015 was still about a third what they were in 1997, and about a fifth what they were at their height in the late 1990s.

Carjacking and truck hijacking have shown fairly erratic trends. As with bank robbery and robbery of cash in transit, it is usually argued that this is because these are highly organised crimes.[74] They require coordination between a number of participants with various skills to appropriately arm and/or disguise the robbers, find the desired vehicles, acquire them, disable their security devices, transport, store, disguise or dismantle, perhaps export abroad and reintegrate them into a sufficiently lucrative market.[75] For trucks, there is the further matter of tracking the desired freight and profitably distributing it. Because of the level of organisation that is involved, effective crime intelligence should be able to make inroads into these crimes, and their trends are considered a good indicator of the effectiveness of police crime intelligence. Further, a relatively large proportion of these crimes is concentrated among a relatively small number of perpetrators, which means that successfully putting just one such network out of operation would have an appreciable impact on the overall rate. The last two decades have also seen the proliferation of a number of key technological developments (e.g. tracking and jamming devices). Truck hijacking numbers are also relatively small – less than 6 per cent as common as house robbery in 2015. All these factors create scope for rapid fluctuation.

Making up the largest volume of aggravated robbery, both in the official figures and as reported in victim surveys, are those incidents that happen in public places, usually on the street. These are not provided by name in the official statistics release, but must instead be derived by subtracting the named subcategories from the total for aggravated robberies. Public or street robbery disproportionately affects poorer communities,[76] is common in informal settlements and around public transport routes, and often targets those who have just received their wages.[77] The rates of aggravated street robbery are not targeted by name for reduction as are those that affect the business sector or are more equally shared with the wealthier. Since it began to be effectively disaggregated in 2003, the street robbery trend has tracked that of aggravated robbery overall, with a long decline turning to an increase since 2012. Public street robberies made up about 80 per cent of recorded aggravated robberies in 2003 and 58 per cent in 2015.

The form of robbery that people perceive to be the most common, and also the one that is most feared, is that which happens at home.[78] The trend in robberies at residential premises has been similar to that for robberies at non-residential premises, which are largely at businesses, but also include religious, educational, cultural, governmental premises, and so on. Of all the crimes involving violence, only three have plausibly risen since we have had their records. House and business robbery are two of them.

After they began to be reported separately in 2003, recorded rates of house robbery rose quite rapidly to 2010, dipped slightly to 2012 – as did many crimes – and have risen quite steadily since. The proportion of recorded aggravated robberies contributed by house robberies has risen from 7 per cent in 2003 to 16 per cent in 2015. Only since 2010 has home robbery been consistently asked about in victimisation surveys. The official rate has gone up about 13 per cent in that time. Oddly, although the proportion of people who said they had reported a home robbery to the police has remained steady at about 60 per cent, the proportion saying that they had been victims of home robbery slightly declined. In other words, fewer people say in victimisation surveys that they were robbed in 2015 than said so in 2010, about the same proportion say they reported it to the police, but the official figures have gone up. This is perplexing. It may well be that despite every effort being made to distinguish the two in the surveys, people aren't very clear about the difference between house robbery and house burglary, which is also called housebreaking. This may also help explain why they consistently claim to fear housebreaking/burglary far more than house robbery, and why the ratio of house burglaries to house robberies as reported in victimisation surveys is about 4:1, when the official figures for them are about 12:1 – despite lower reporting rates for burglaries. Further, three times as many people say they have experienced a home robbery as those who say they have had a car stolen, when the official figures suggest almost exactly the reverse, and again despite higher reporting rates for car thefts. In this case, perhaps because house robbery is such an emotive event, victimisation survey data seems not to be of much use.

The recorded rates of robberies at non-residential premises have almost tripled since 2003 – the single largest rise of any violent crime. They were at 12 per 100 000 in 2003 and reached 35 by 2015. They have gone from making up 3 per cent of all aggravated robberies to 15 per cent. For all the media concern with mall robberies, it must be noted that the overwhelming majority of business robberies involve small and relatively informal businesses.[79] They have not been asked about in victimisation surveys.

All of these trends in different forms of robbery begin to form a coherent picture. It does seem likely to us that the overall rate of robbery in 2015 is lower, or at least not significantly higher, than it was in 1995. The increasing rates of the first decade after 1994 may well at least partly have reflected increasing reporting. The overall decline at least since then seems to have been driven primarily by declines in relatively disorganised robberies on the street and, to a lesser extent (because less numerous), carjacking. House and business robberies remain relatively rare but seem to have been increasing for the last decade, and they have, since 2012, been joined in their increase by the much more numerous street robbery.

The instrumentalisation of violence

The patterns of the last 20 years suggest that the traditionally more expressive forms of violence have declined a good deal, that the more instrumental forms of violence have declined much more slowly, if at all, that increases in robbery at homes and businesses have contributed most to the sluggishness of the decline of robbery, and that the more numerous category of aggravated street robbery may have risen since 2012. Robbery seems to have become more frequent relative to assault, and more of it has moved away from cars and off the streets and instead into homes and businesses. Violence has become increasingly instrumentalised. This may be a positive sign, as these crimes may well be more feasibly prevented or deterred. It is also a positive sign in its own right that assault rates seem to be so much lower than they were. This may represent improvement in an old national culture of violent interpersonal conflict resolution.

On the other hand, this change in the context of violence and policing may be one of the reasons why fear of crime has not tracked with the decline in murder. Some crimes weigh heavier than others in people's conceptions of safety, even though they may on some objective scale be less 'serious'.[80] The prospect of violence in the course of a robbery may well be far more frightening than that in the course of an interpersonal dispute.

Another insight that can be drawn from the relative trends in recorded rates and self-reported victimisation rates is about faith in the police. The patterns in robbery are harder to untangle, but those in assault are matched in other crimes subject to considerable discretion in reporting, namely, non-violent property crime. Just less than half the over 2 million crimes the police recorded in 2015 were non-violent property crimes. The single most frequently recorded type are 'all thefts not mentioned elsewhere', which is those that don't involve breaking into a building, or vehicles, livestock, commercial crime or shoplifting. 'All thefts not mentioned elsewhere' is an extremely broad category, but although it does reflect losses worth many millions due to highly organised criminal syndicates, according to the SAPS the majority are 'petty thefts' of cash or small items like mobile phones and jewellery.[81] Its recorded trend shows a large increase of more than a third, peaking around 2003, followed by a slowing decline to end in 2015 at a rate about a third lower than that in 1995. The victimisation rate reflected in surveys has at the same time declined by over a half, and has done so steadily from at least 1998 – certainly with no peak from the late 1990s.[82] Instead, the period sees a rise in the proportion of incidents reported to the police, from 28 per cent in 1998 to 42 per cent in 2003,[83] declining again to about 34 per cent in 2015.[84] The reporting rates in different crimes peaked in different years, but many rose significantly in the first decade after 1994 and have fallen since.

Much of the apparent crime wave of the late 1990s and early 2000s was not corroborated by self-reported victimisation rates, and appears to have been the product of increasing reporting to the police. Changes in opinions on how the police are faring can also be read in the responses to other survey questions. The percentage of survey respondents who were satisfied with the policing in their area went from 38 per cent in 1998 to 52 per cent in 2003.[85] By 2007, it had started slipping down to 49 per cent.[86] The question format has since changed, but the proportion of satisfied households has continued slipping by two or three percentage points in every successive survey.[87] Interestingly, other surveys suggest that this decline has not been matched in attitudes about police legitimacy.[88] The police do not seem to be less trusted than they were, even though people are less inclined to report a number of crimes. Fear or dislike of the police is not the reason for non-reporting; it is largely a sense that police either can or will do nothing about it anyway.[89] The 'democracy bulge' in crime reporting appears to have passed. People seem to have been disappointed.

A final matter that may be of interest is that whereas the context of assault has changed little, there has been a change in that of robbery. The proportion of robbery victims who said they knew who robbed them in 2003 was 19 per cent, and in 2007 was 22 per cent.[90] In 2015, it was about 38 per cent.[91] Although still a minority, twice as many people know the perpetrators of their robbery as did in 2003. This effect seems to have been largely concentrated in the Western Cape, in which more than half of victims now say they knew their robber, and most of these say they knew them by name or by face.[92] An increase in predation on familiars is a matter for concern. Targeting acquaintances for robbery is highly risky unless there is a sense of impunity within a community. Breakdowns in the normal protective factors of familiarity have in other places been found to be related to the role of drugs, of gangs and of firearms.[93] We would argue that gangs and other drug-related criminal governance in the Western Cape are driving this change, as well as the area's disproportionate increase in violence overall. In the next chapter, we will touch on what this might mean in the South African context.

Conclusion: what makes crime go down?

Although the crime statistics everywhere, and especially here in South Africa, are plagued by problems, they have the potential to tell us a great deal about the past and present organisation of our social world. Neither the rate of crime nor its distribution is random. The trends over time and the patterns in space can tell us things we might otherwise have missed. Without them we cannot make good decisions or build good strategies. There is another thing that crime statistics can do: they can help inform an understanding of the future and of how the shape of that future might be determined. Looking at the last two decades in South Africa, we can point to two things that might help to bring crime down, one that won't and one that is imperative if we want to make progress at pulling rates of

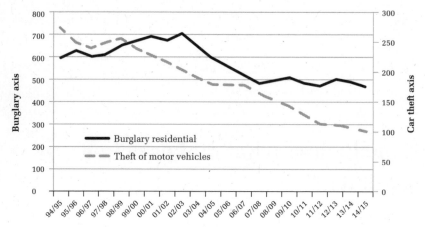

Figure 14: Recorded rates of residential burglary and vehicle theft

violence below levels that, despite major improvement, are still among the highest in the world.

Two of the crimes that have seen clear declines in their recorded rates in the last 20 years have been residential burglary and car theft. Their trends are shown in Figure 14.

Vehicle theft rates have dropped by almost two-thirds. We can give credence to this because, at almost 90 per cent, car theft has the highest reporting rates of any property crime. In raw numbers and despite an increasing proportion of households owning a car,[1] an increasing population and a high and steady proportion of victims saying they reported their car thefts to the police,[2] about half as many cars were reported stolen in 2015 as were in 1995. Victimisation surveys also confirm the trend, and if anything suggest there is a slight underestimation.[3] How can we make sense of this? The biggest driver is probably a combination between technological and behavioural change. In 2003, 5 per cent of people said they had taken measures to protect their car from crime; in 2007, it was 15 per cent; in 2015, 29 per cent. The circumstances around vehicle thefts span a broader spectrum than those for carjacking, in some cases involving specialised syndicates targeting high-value cars for resale, and in others entirely opportunistic theft of older, less secure cars for parts.[4] As the security on high-end cars has improved, with driver cooperation increasingly required, relatively opportunistic and unskilled theft of these vehicles has become far more difficult. This has probably put some upward pressure on hijackings,[5] although, as we've seen from the overall downward trend in those, it can't have done so to a very great extent. As a result of technological change, an increasing proportion of car theft is disorganised and involves relatively low-end vehicles. It has been said that some of the decline in the demand for these may be due to a decline in the market for older models or parts.[6] Vehicle thefts have also fallen in this same period in other parts of the world.[7] Immobilisers, alarms and tracking devices have made car theft much harder and riskier than it used to be.

Another crime that has declined is residential burglary. This is the crime that people in the country report in victim surveys that they most fear and also think is most common.[8] Its recorded rates rose slightly with many crimes to 2003, then fell and have fluctuated in a fairly narrow band since about 2006, for a total reduction over the period of about 20 per cent. The reduction in self-reported victimisation rates has been about 30 per cent, and there has been only a slight reduction in reporting rates.[9] At least some of this reduction is likely also the result of technological and behavioural change. Many households have become more careful and better at securing their homes with alarm systems, armed response, burglar bars, and so on. This is known as target hardening. The proportion who say they have taken such measures has increased from 39 per cent in 2003 to 52 per cent in 2015. The upward trend in house robbery does suggest that target hardening may be playing a role, as it is increasingly necessary for residents to be present to provide access to the house and its most valuable property. The pattern in recorded rates of non-residential burglary has been lower throughout but almost identical. Technological and behavioural changes have probably helped drive reductions in these crimes, but the declines have slowed or even stalled in recent years. So has the growth in the proportion of households that have taken steps to secure their spaces.[10] If the proportion of vehicles, houses and businesses that take steps to secure themselves continues to grow, we can probably expect to see further reductions in these crimes. There is of course a relationship between the capacity to protect oneself and one's belongings and wealth.[11] The relatively well-off, at least in urban areas, may have hardened their targets about as much as money can feasibly buy, but there remains major scope for securing the rest of the country. On the other hand, target hardening is not infallible or always as effective as people may hope.[12] More importantly, constant escalation of the fortress mentality – the heightening of walls, barring of windows and privatising of security – is not only unsustainable in the long run but may also be exacerbating exactly the conditions that drive crime rates up.[13]

Another trend we should consider is that in drug-related crime. Drug-related need tops the list for why most people think perpetrators commit at least property crimes.[14] Although many more crimes, including murders, may be in some way related to illegal drugs, in the police figures this term refers only to those that revolve around them directly, that is, their production, distribution and possession. The official rates of drug-related crime have seen more increase over the last two decades than any other crime type. They stayed fairly steady to 2003, then increased fivefold in a little over a decade. As it is a police-detected crime, it is hard to know what to make of its recorded rates.

The standard argument about drugs in South Africa goes that apartheid isolation may have served to constrain the import of foreign drugs, and that since then there has been a major increase in the volumes of drugs flowing into and through the country as a result of the confluence of its reintegration into the global community, the expansion of cross-border trade, long and porous borders, convenience as a transshipment point between Africa and Europe, and internal social dislocation. Other evidence does suggest that there has been an increase in the volume of illegal drugs in the country, but it isn't clear to what extent.[15] There are certainly areas where it has seemed that drug production, distribution and use have steadily increased.[16] Despite the more than 1.7 million drug-related charges that have been laid in the last decade, and the tons of drugs confiscated and destroyed, there are probably far more illegal drugs in the country today than there were 20 years ago. This doesn't seem to have been spread equally through the country. At more than three times the national average and more than twice the average for the major metros, the rate of drug-related crime in Cape Town is a huge outlier. It has gone in the last decade from a clear lead among the major cities to an overwhelming one.

The relationship between drugs and other crime is complex. It could be that Cape Town has seen high and growing rates of drug abuse, and that this is driving other forms of crime for any number of reasons. It could also be that police action against drugs has destabilised drug markets, leading to more violent competition between the criminal organisations that profit from them. Regardless of the mechanism, it is striking that this same period has seen Cape Town's rates of some other crimes also escalate out of any proportion to the other major metros. Its murder rate has risen far faster than the national average or the major city average. It has in recent years gone from the middle of the pack of cities to a clear lead. If Cape Town were excluded from the national total, the national murder rate rise of the last three years would be almost halved. See Figure 15 for Cape Town's murder rate relative to the average for the other large metro areas.

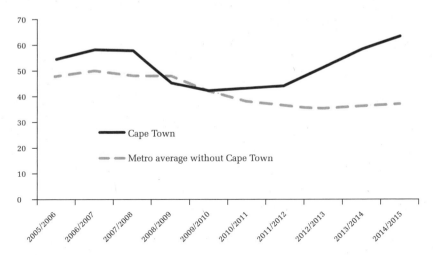

Figure 15: Murder rates in Cape Town compared to the other metros

Over and above the crime drivers it likely shares with the other metros, Cape Town has a serious problem with drugs and gangs. It shows no sign of abating and will probably continue to drive murder rates up. This should serve as a warning to the rest of the country that whatever the progress on broader social issues, locally specific factors, such as the entrenchment of a violent drug market, may rapidly reverse any hard-won previous gains in the reduction of violence.

Finally, the insight of the long term is that levels of violence have recovered from the peak around transition and returned to about the levels of the 1970s. The reduction in violence since 1994 has been significant, but it has not been the result of any fundamental restructuring away from the conditions that make South Africa a high-violence country. The increase of the last three years suggests that we are at a crossroads. For the first

179

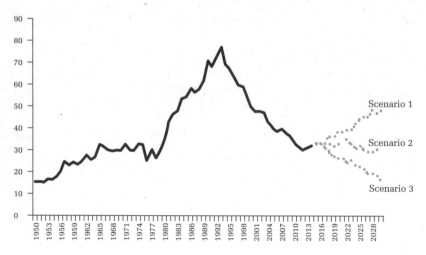

Figure 16: Proposed murder rate scenarios in context

time since transition, the murder rate is no longer going down by default. Getting it down further will require finally grappling with the circumstances that propelled us into this band. There are a number of ways things can go from here. While the sketching of scenarios brings with it a range of challenges, we use it here as a device to suggest what a set of alternative futures may look like for murder (see Figure 16).

As our explanation above has indicated, like many other analysts we are concerned by the recent upswing in murder, given that it is a reversal of a two-decade decline. Scenario 1 would see an increase of South Africa's murder rate on its current upward trajectory. This scenario would be most likely in a context of an ongoing failure to address the key underlying drivers of violence plus increasing political, economic and social instability, and declining state legitimacy. Increases

180

in murder in Cape Town in particular, with its specific set of problems around drugs and gangs, would, as we have suggested above, continue to be a major contributor. However, the influence of conflict around drug markets and organised crime could spread to other cities.

Scenario 2 suggests that things will not get dramatically worse, but nor will they get better with any speed. Murder levels could fluctuate in a band at about this same high level for years. Declines in some parts of the country will be matched by increases in others, and homicides will continue to be increasingly associated with aggravated robbery. In our view, without strong policy action, this is currently the most likely scenario. The long decline in murder may have largely stabilised at the point that reflects the cocktail of violence-inducing factors that characterise our society. In this scenario, murder may slowly decline further, but this will be a long-term process, taking perhaps another decade to drop out of the very high violence band. That means thousands of lives lost. We can and must do better.

Scenario 3 provides an indication of what we may be able to achieve. This would represent a historic step in a society so long characterised by violence. We think that a concerted effort could make it possible. It would require better policing, particularly around aggravated robbery. It would require working to restore and build faith in the police, to encourage a sense of legitimacy, lawfulness and trust in the relationship between state and society. It would require focusing resources and problem-solving initiative in that handful of places that host the very highest levels of violence. More than anything, however, we believe it would require a massive effort to improve the life chances of marginalised young people, especially young men. The hotspots for violence are as much social as they are geographic. The scale of what is required is the equivalent of Roosevelt's New Deal for a South African context. Investing in the creation of skills, jobs and options for non-violent access to resources, status and dignity for those most at risk benefits the entire society. The extreme spatial and socioeconomic exclusion of the majority of the population from opportunities for the stable, dignified, prosperous life enjoyed by the few is not sustainable. South Africa cannot become a radically less violent place until it becomes a radically less unequal one.

The scenarios are simple. If we do nothing, levels of violence may fluctuate at a high level or perhaps creep down incrementally over years. If we do nothing and also see such aggravating factors as increased social instability and the establishment of a virulent and chaotic drug market, levels of violence may again rise to see us rejoin the countries in Central and Latin America at the very highest ranks of murder. If we begin to make bigger inroads into repairing the structural damage wrought from especially the mid-1950s, we may be able to do as the majority of the world does but what few living in South Africa today can remember: live in a country that allows its people the simple luxury of a natural death.

Appendix: the numbers

We have compiled these figures and rates from a number of different statistical releases and annual reports by the SAP/ SAPS. At various points over the period, they have changed their method of reporting and the dates of annual coverage, so these may not to the digit match those in another source.

Official police recorded murder figures

1911	37	1931		1951	1983	1971	7463	1991	14693	2011	15893
1912	156	1932	652	1952	2002	1972	6920	1992	16067	2012	15554
1913		1933		1953	2245	1973	7210	1993	17467	2013	16213
1914		1934	794	1954	2289	1974	8262	1994	26832	2014	17023
1915		1935	877	1955	2486	1975	8534	1995	26637	2015	17805
1916	392	1936	883	1956	2959	1976	5909	1996	25782		
1917		1937	1117	1957	3583	1977	7478	1997	24588		
1918	403	1938	1011	1958	3425	1978	5863	1998	24875		
1919	474	1939	1024	1959	3711	1979	6839	1999	23823		
1920	480	1940	1184	1960	3812	1980	8263	2000	21683		
1921	513	1941	1178	1961	4081	1981	7434	2001	21180		
1922	513	1942		1962	4753	1982	8084	2002	21738		
1923	554	1943	1384	1963	4464	1983	8573	2003	21553		
1924		1944		1964	4792	1984	9462	2004	19824		
1925	502	1945	1469	1965	5949	1985	8959	2005	18793		
1926	495	1946	1371	1966	6043	1986	9665	2006	18455		
1927	471	1947	1570	1967	5800	1987	9800	2007	19106		
1928	578	1948	1733	1968	5825	1988	10631	2008	18400		
1929	616	1949	1747	1969	6054	1989	11750	2009	18084		
1930	556	1950	1922	1970	6564	1990	15109	2010	16767		

Estimated murder rates per 100 000 in police jurisdiction

1911	0.6	1931		1951	15	1971	33	1991	68	2011	31
1912	2.6	1932	8	1952	15	1972	30	1992	73	2012	30
1913		1933		1953	16	1973	30	1993	78	2013	31
1914		1934	9	1954	16	1974	33	1994	69	2014	32
1915		1935	10	1955	18	1975	32	1995	67	2015	33
1916	6.0	1936	10	1956	21	1976	25	1996	64		
1917		1937	11	1957	24	1977	30	1997	60		
1918	6.0	1938	10	1958	23	1978	26	1998	59		
1919	7.0	1939	10	1959	24	1979	29	1999	55		
1920	7.0	1940	11	1960	23	1980	34	2000	50		
1921	7.4	1941	11	1961	24	1981	43	2001	48		
1922	7.3	1942		1962	28	1982	46	2002	48		
1923	7.7	1943	13	1963	25	1983	48	2003	47		
1924		1944		1964	27	1984	54	2004	43		
1925	6.7	1945	13	1965	32	1985	54	2005	40		
1926	6.6	1946	12	1966	32	1986	58	2006	39		
1927	6.1	1947	14	1967	30	1987	56	2007	40		
1928	7.3	1948	15	1968	29	1988	58	2008	38		
1929	7.8	1949	14	1969	30	1989	62	2009	36		
1930	6.9	1950	15	1970	30	1990	71	2010	33		

Other crime rates per 100 000

	Attempted murder	Assault GBH	Common assault	Rape and attempted rape	Total sexual offences	Aggravated robbery	Other/common robbery	Car-jacking	Truck hi-jacking*	Robbery of CIT*	Bank robbery*	House robbery
1995	69	556	516	112		219	84					
1996	68	564	521	122		195	115					
1997	70	570	500	127		163	125	32	3694	410	642	
1998	68	570	489	128		178	133	32	4296	230	497	
1999	70	566	485	118		221	155	38	5773	214	476	
2000	65	608	539	120		230	174	35	5506	224	458	
2001	64	630	570	122		260	207	34	4769	234	447	
2002	70	589	584	122		261	201	35	3792	162	432	
2003	79	586	622	115		279	223	32	3333	238	356	
2004	65	560	605	121		288	206	30	986	374	127	20
2005	52	530	570	115	142	270	193	26	901	192	54	20
2006	43	474	473	114	147	251	156	27	930	220	58	20
2007	41	449	431	118	141	262	146	28	829	383	59	21
2008	38	427	400		133	242	132	29	892	467	129	26
2009	37	408	385		128	245	119	30	1245	394	144	30
2010	34	406	388		140	226	113	28	1437	386	102	37
2011	30	388	362		133	199	107	21	1412	358	93	37
2012	29	371	349		128	196	102	18	999	290	39	33
2013	31	354	328		117	202	102	19	821	182	35	33
2014	32	344	313		116	225	101	21	943	145	7	34
2015	32	338	299		107	239	102	24	991	145	21	36

* These crimes provided as raw figures rather than as rates per 100 000.

Business robbery	Street robbery	Burglary residential	Burglary non-residential	Common assault	Theft of motor vehicle and motorcycle	Theft out of or from motor vehicle	All theft not mentioned elsewhere	Arson	Malicious damage to property	Drug-related crime	Driving under the influence of alcohol or drugs	Illegal possession of firearms and ammunition
		596	226	516	273	473	996	28	318	118	66	28
		629	221	521	249	485	979	24	328	99	58	31
		603	215	500	240	430	925	25	320	100	60	31
		611	219	489	249	435	969	24	307	103	70	33
		653	225	485	256	453	1051	24	308	94	60	35
		673	216	539	239	454	1153	22	312	101	61	36
		694	209	570	229	459	1281	21	319	103	58	34
		675	194	584	216	445	1287	20	325	118	55	35
		704	163	622	205	431	1365	20	346	118	49	35
12	210	645	139	605	190	371	1307	19	341	135	54	36
8	228	587	119	570	178	316	1141	17	321	179	64	33
7	214	549	114	473	180	291	891	15	298	199	69	28
9	190	515	121	431	178	256	845	15	292	216	79	29
14	190	484	128	400	164	227	792	14	274	223	99	27
20	158	495	141	385	153	220	781	13	265	236	113	28
28	145	508	142	388	142	239	717	13	258	268	125	29
29	128	485	135	362	126	240	710	12	241	296	131	28
29	113	474	136	349	114	251	719	12	232	342	135	28
31	112	500	141	328	111	266	683	11	228	395	136	28
31	115	490	139	313	107	271	686	10	223	492	132	29
35	130	470	138	299	102	269	668	9	223	494	127	28

Notes

Introduction

1 Gavin Silber and Nathan Geffen, 'Race, Class and Violent Crime in South Africa', *South African Crime Quarterly*, 30 (2009), pp. 35–43.
2 Zenobia Ismail, *Is Crime Dividing the Rainbow Nation? Fear of Crime in South Africa, Afrobarometer Briefing Paper 96*, 2010.
3 National Treasury, 'Budget Highlights Card', 2016. Available at www.treasury.gov.za/documents/national budget/2016. Accessed 26 February 2016.
4 Nivashni Nair, 'First Food, Then Private Security', *Times Live*, 20 July 2015. Available at www.timeslive.co.za. Accessed 29 March 2016.
5 South African Police Service, *Annual Report 2014/2015*, 2015, p. 308.
6 Private Security Industry Regulatory Authority, *Annual Report 2013/2014*, 31 July 2014, p. 9. Available at www.psira.co.za/psira/. Accessed 29 March 2016.
7 Department of Correctional Services, *Annual Report 2014/2015*, 2015, p. 78.
8 Department of Justice and Constitutional Development, *Annual Report 2014/2015*, 2015, p. 242.
9 Brett Bowman and Garth Stevens, 'Injury Costing in South Africa: The State of the Sector', in *Crime, violence and injury in South Africa: developments and challenges*, ed. by S Suffla, A van Niekerk (Cape Town: MRC, 2002), p. 7.
10 Deepali M Patel and Rachel M Taylor, Rapporteurs; Forum on Global Violence Prevention; Board on Global Health, *Social and Economic Costs*

of Violence: Workshop Summary, 2012, p. 37. Available at www.nap.edu/
openbook.php?record_id=13254. Accessed 29 March 2016.

11 Erik Alda and Jose Cuesta, 'A Comprehensive Estimation of Costs of Crime
in South Africa and Its Implications for Effective Policy Making', *Journal
of International Development*, 23 (2011), pp. 926–35.

12 Sapa, 'Cable Theft Costs South Africa R5bn a Year: Mthethwa', *Times Live*,
20 November 2012.

13 See e.g. Christopher Stone, *Crime, Justice, and Growth in South Africa:
Toward a Plausible Contribution from Criminal Justice to Economic
Growth, Economic Growth Working Papers*, 2006, p. 9.

14 Silvana Patriarca, *Numbers and Nationhood: Writing Statistics in
Nineteenth-Century Italy* (Cambridge: Cambridge University Press, 1996).

15 Mike Maguire, 'Criminal Statistics and the Construction of Crime',
in *The Oxford Handbook of Criminology*, ed. by Mike Maguire, Rod
Morgan and Robert Reiner, 5th edn (Oxford: Oxford University Press,
2012), p. 207.

16 Jean Comaroff and John Comaroff, 'Figuring Crime: Quantifacts and the
Production of the Un/real', *Public Culture*, 18 (2006), pp. 209–46 (p. 210).

17 George S Rigakos, 'Risk Society and Actual Criminology: Prospects for a
Critical Discourse', *Canadian Journal of Criminology*, 1999, pp. 137–50.

18 United Nations, *Manual for the Development of a System of Criminal
Justice Statistics* (New York, 2003), p. 1.

19 Julia Hornberger, 'From General to Commissioner to General – On the
Popular State of Policing in South Africa', *Law and Social Inquiry*, 38
(2013), pp. 598–614.

20 RS Nickerson, 'Confirmation Bias: A Ubiquitous Phenomenon in Many
Guises', *Review of General Psychology*, 2 (1998), pp. 175–220.

21 Julie Berg, 'The Rise of "tik" and the Crime Rate', *South African Journal of
Criminal Justice*, 18 (2006), pp. 306–28 (p. 306).

22 Morten Jerven, *Poor Numbers: How We Are Misled by African Development
Statistics and What to Do about It* (Ithaca: Cornell University Press, 2013).

23 Comaroff and Comaroff.

24 This is evidenced by the fact that the main reason for not reporting a
crime to the police is the perception that the police could or would not
do anything about it. See Statistics South Africa, *Victims of Crime Survey
2014/2015*, 2015, p. 67.

25 Nils Christie, *Crime Control as Industry: Towards GULAGS, Western Style*,
3rd edn (London: Routledge, 2000), p. 22.

26 See e.g. Darrell Steffensmeier, Jeffery Ulmer and John Kramer, 'The
Interaction of Race, Gender, and Age in Criminal Sentencing: The
Punishment Cost of Being Young, Black, and Male', *Criminology*, 36
(1998), pp. 763–98; George S Bridges and Sara Steen, 'Racial Disparities
in Official Assessments of Juvenile Offenders: Attributional Stereotypes
Mediating Mechanisms', *American Sociological Review*, 63 (1998), pp.
554–70; Theodore R Curry, Gang Lee and SF Rodriguez, 'Does Victim
Gender Increase Sentence Severity? Further Explorations of Gender
Dynamics and Sentencing Outcomes', *Crime & Delinquency*, 50 (2004),
pp. 319–43; S Fernando Rodriguez, Theodore R Curry and Gang Lee,

'Gender Difference in Criminal Sentencing: Do Effects Vary across Violent, Property, and Drug Offenses?', *Social Science Quarterly*, 87 (2006), pp 318–39; David B Mustard, 'Racial, Ethnic, and Gender Disparities in Sentencing: Evidence from the US Federal Courts', *The Journal of Law & Economics*, 44 (2001), pp. 285–314.

27 Statistics South Africa, *Victims of Crime Survey 2014/2015*, p. 2.

28 Benjamin Roberts, 'Age of Hope or Anxiety? Dynamics of the Fear of Crime in South Africa', *HSRC Review*, 6 (2008), pp. 9–10.

29 See e.g. DC May, NE Rader and S Goodrum, 'A Gendered Assessment of the Threat of Victimization: Examining Gender Differences in Fear of Crime, Perceived Risk, Avoidance, and Defensive Behaviors', *Criminal Justice Review*, 35 (2010), pp. 159–82; Rachel Pain, 'Gender, Race, Age and Fear in the City', *Urban Studies*, 38 (2001), pp. 899–913; Marian Tulloch, 'The Meaning of Age Differences in the Fear of Crime', *British Journal of Criminology*, 40 (2000), pp. 451–67.

30 Charlotte Lemanski, 'Global Cities in the South: Deepening Social and Spatial Polarisation in Cape Town', *Cities*, 24 (2007), pp. 448–61.

31 See e.g. Jon Gunnar Bernburg, Marvin D Krohn and Craig J Rivera, 'Official Labeling, Criminal Embeddedness, and Subsequent Delinquency: A Longitudinal Test of Labeling Theory', *Journal of Research in Crime and Delinquency*, 43 (2006), pp. 67–88.

32 Comaroff and Comaroff, p. 239.

33 Stone Sizani, 'Statistics Show Crime Remains a Serious Challenge', Politicsweb, 29 September 2015. Available at www.politicsweb.co.za. Accessed 29 March 2016.

34 Richard Mamabolo, 'Statistics Don't Show the Whole Crime Picture – Popcru', Politicsweb, 5 October 2015. Available at www.politicsweb.co.za. Accessed 29 March 2016.

35 Albert Mncwango, 'SAPS Crime Statistics a Far Cry from Current Reality', press release, 29 September 2015. Available at www.ifp.org.za. Accessed 29 March 2016.

36 Pieter Groenewald, 'Don't Be Fooled by Crime Statistics', Politicsweb, 29 September 2015. Available at www.politicsweb.co.za. Accessed 29 March 2016.

37 Dianne Kohler Barnard, 'Crime Stats: National Government's Failings Need to Be Addressed to Keep South Africans Safe', *DA News*, 29 September 2015. Available at www.da.org.za. Accessed 29 March 2016.

38 Juran van den Heever, 'Leaderless Police Service to Blame for Crime Rate – Solidarity', Politicsweb, 29 September 2015. Available at www. politicsweb.co.za. Accessed 29 March 2016.

39 Simon Fredericks and Dirk Van Zyl Smit, *Criminological Statistics* (University of Cape Town, Institute of Criminology, 1984).

40 Mary Shaw, Helena Tunstall and Danny Dorling, 'Increasing Inequalities in Risk of Murder in Britain: Trends in the Demographic and Spatial Distribution of Murder, 1981–2000', *Health and Place*, 11 (2005), pp. 45–54 (p. 45).

41 Antoinette Louw, 'Surviving the Transition: Trends and Perceptions of Crime in South Africa', *Social Indicators Research*, 41 (1997), pp. 137–68 (p. 138).

1 What are crime statistics?

1 David Gadd, Susanne Karstedt and Steven F Messner, 'Editorial Introduction', in *The Sage Handbook of Criminological Research Methods* (London: Sage Publications, 2012), pp. 3–4.

2 Sandra Walklate, *Criminology: The Basics*, 2nd edn (Abingdon, UK: Routledge, 2011), p. 30.

3 Keith Bottomley and Clive Coleman, *Understanding Crime Rates: Police and Public Roles in the Production of Official Statistics* (Farnborough: Gower, 1981), p. 12.

4 Janne Kivivuori, *Discovery of Hidden Crime: Self-Report Delinquency Surveys in Criminal Policy Context* (Oxford: Oxford University Press, 2011), p. 1.

5 Jan van Dijk, 'Approximating the Truth about Crime: Comparing Crime Data Based on General Population Surveys with Police Figures of Recorded Crimes', in *Comparing Crime Data in Europe: Official Statistics and Survey Based Data*, ed. by Philippe Robert (Brussels: VUBPRESS, 2009), p. 14.

6 Antony Altbeker, 'Puzzling Statistics: Is South Africa Really the World's Crime Capital?', *South African Crime Quarterly*, 2005, pp. 1–8 (p. 6).

7 Silber and Geffen.

8 Jean Redpath, 'Using Data to Make a Difference through Victimisation Surveys', *South African Crime Quarterly*, 32 (2010), p. 10.

9 Redpath, p. 10.

10 Marcelo F Aebi, Martin Killias and Cynthia Tavares, 'Comparing Crime Rates: The International Crime (Victim) Survey, the European Sourcebook of Crime and Criminal Justice Statistics, and Interpol Statistics', *International Journal of Comparative Criminology*, 2 (2002), pp. 22–37 (p. 31).

11 David Cantor and JP Lynch, 'Self-Report Surveys as Measures of Crime and Criminal Victimization', *Criminal Justice*, 2000, pp. 85–138 (pp. 88–89).

12 Van Dijk, p. 15.

13 Walklate, p. 30.

14 Bottomley and Coleman, pp. 4–5.

15 Adrian Smith, *Crime Statistics: An Independent Review Carried out for the Secretary of State for the Home Department* (London, 2006), p. 11.

16 Julie Berg and Wilfried Scharf, 'Crime Statistics in South Africa 1994–2003', *South African Criminal Justice Journal*, 17 (2004), pp. 57–78 (p. 66).

17 Bottomley and Coleman, p. 7.

18 Walklate, p. 30.

19 Image courtesy of Walklate, p. 33.

20 Nigel Walker, *Crimes, Courts and Figures: An Introduction to Criminal Statistics* (London: Penguin Books, 1971), pp. 24–25.

21 See e.g. Rachel Jewkes and Naeema Abrahams, 'The Epidemiology of Rape and Sexual Coercion in South Africa: An Overview', *Social Science & Medicine*, 55 (2002), pp. 1231–44.

22 P Knepper, 'Falling Crime Rates: What Happened Last Time', *Theoretical Criminology*, 19 (2015), pp. 59–76 (pp. 59–60).

23 Manuel Eisner and Amy Nivette, 'How to Reduce the Global Homicide

Rate to 2 per 100,000 by 2060', in *The Future of Criminology*, ed. by Rolf Loeber and Brandon C Welsh (Oxford: Oxford University Press, 2012), pp. 219–25.

24 Anthony Braga, Andrew V Papachristos and David Hureau, 'The Effects of Hot Spots Policing on Crime', *Campbell Systematic Reviews*, 8 (2012). Available at campbellcollaboration.org/lib/project/24/. Accessed 29 March 2016.

25 David Weisburd and others, 'The Effects of Problem-Oriented Policing on Crime and Disorder', *Campbell Systematic Reviews*, 14 (2008). Available at campbellcollaboration.org/lib/project/46/. Accessed 29 March 2016.

26 Jonathan Jackson and others, 'Why Do People Comply with the Law?', *British Journal of Criminology*, 52 (2012), pp. 1051–71.

27 Andrew Faull, 'Missing the Target: When Measuring Performance Undermines Police Effectiveness', *South African Crime Quarterly*, 31 (2010), pp. 19–25.

28 Faull, 'Missing the Target', p. 22.

29 Faull, 'Missing the Target'.

30 David Bruce, '"The Ones in the Pile Were the Ones Going Down": the Reliability of Violent Crime Statistics', *South African Crime Quarterly*, 31 (2010), pp. 9–17.

31 J David Goodman, 'New York Police Commissioner and Predecessor Spar over Accuracy of Crime Data', *New York Times*, 29 December 2015. Available at www.nytimes.com. Accessed 12 January 2016.

32 Donald J Black, 'Production of Crime Rates', *American Sociological Review*, 35 (1970), pp. 733–48.

33 Lillian Artz and Dee Smythe, 'Losing Ground? Making Sense of Attrition in Rape Cases', *South African Crime Quarterly*, 22 (2007), pp. 13–20; Dee Smythe, *Rape Unresolved: Policing Sexual Offences in South Africa* (Cape Town: University of Cape Town Press, 2015).

34 South African Police Service, *Annual Performance Plan 2010/2011*, 2011.

35 Chris De Kock, Anine Kriegler and Mark Shaw, *A Citizen's Guide to SAPS Crime Statistics: 1994 to 2015*, University of Cape Town, Centre for Criminology, 2015, pp. 15–16.

36 David Masiloane, 'Crime Statistics: A Critical Discussion of More Policeable and Less Policeable Crimes', *Acta Criminologica: Southern African Journal of Criminology*, 27 (2014), pp. 129–43.

37 Statistics South Africa, *Victims of Crime Survey 2014/2015*, p. 67.

38 Statistics South Africa, *Victims of Crime Survey 2014/2015*, p. 41.

39 Commission of Inquiry into Allegations of Police Inefficiency and a Breakdown in Relations between SAPS and the Community in Khayelitsha, *Towards a Safer Khayelitsha*, 2014, p. 60.

40 Andrew Faull, 'Performance Measurement in Police Agencies', 2014.

41 Ndifuna Ukwazi did do an admirable job with their analysis of the 2012/2013 SAPS annual report.

42 David Bruce and Rachel Neild, 'The Police That We Want: A Handbook for Oversight of the Police in South Africa', Open Society Justice Initiative, 2005, p. 44.

43 South African Police Service, *Annual Report 2014/2015*, pp. 131, 132, 153.

44 Ted Leggett, 'The Sieve Effect: South Africa's Conviction Rates in Perspective', *South African Crime Quarterly*, 2003, pp. 11–14.
45 Leggett, 'The Sieve Effect', p. 12.
46 South African Law Commission, *Conviction Rates and Other Outcomes of Crimes Reported in Eight South African Police Areas*, 2001, p. 8.
47 South African Law Commission, p. 18.
48 South African Law Commission, p. 22.
49 South African Police Service, *Annual Report 2014/2015*, p. 200.
50 South African Police Service, *Annual Report 2014/2015*, p. 201.
51 South African Police Service, *Annual Report 2014/2015*, p. 201.
52 South African Police Service, *Annual Report 2014/2015*, p. 190.
53 South African Police Service, *Annual Report 2014/2015*, p. 190.
54 South African Police Service, *Annual Report 2014/2015*, p. 203.
55 United Kingdom Ministry of Justice, 'Criminal Justice Statistics Quarterly Update to March 2013 England and Wales', 2014, p. 22.

2 The South African crime statistics context

1 Maguire, p. 206.
2 Robert C Williamson, 'Crime in South Africa: Some Aspects of Causes and Treatment', *Journal of Criminal Law, Criminology & Police Science*, 48 (1957), pp. 185–92 (p. 186).
3 David Bruce, *New Wine from an Old Cask? The South African Police Service and the Process of Transformation*, paper presented at John Jay College of Criminal Justice, New York, 9 May 2002. Available at www.csvr. org.za. Accessed 29 March 2016.
4 Gregory D Breetzke, 'Understanding the Magnitude and Extent of Crime in Post-Apartheid South Africa', *Social Identities*, 18 (2012), pp. 299–315 (p. 301).
5 Gail Super, 'The Spectacle of Crime in the "New" South Africa: A Historical Perspective (1976–2004)', *British Journal of Criminology*, 50 (2010), pp. 165–84 (p. 8).
6 Breetzke, p. 301.
7 Philip H Frankel, 'South Africa: The Politics of Police Control', *Comparative Politics*, 12 (1980), pp. 481–99 (p. 487).
8 Ted Leggett, 'Just Another Miracle: A Decade of Crime and Justice in Democratic South Africa', *Social Research*, 72 (2005), pp. 581–604 (pp. 587–588).
9 Peter Gastrow and Mark Shaw, 'In Search of Safety: Police Transformation Public Responses in South Africa', *Daedalus*, 130 (2001), pp. 259–75 (p. 264).
10 Breetzke, p. 302.
11 Chandré Gould, 'Editorial: Memory and Forgetting: How Meta-Narratives about the Past Overshadow the Future', *South African Crime Quarterly*, 2014, pp. 4–6.
12 Gastrow and Shaw, p. 261.

13 See e.g. Gary Kynoch, 'Crime, Conflict and Politics in Transition-Era South Africa', *African Affairs*, 104 (2005), pp. 493–514; Gary Kynoch, 'Reassessing Transition Violence: Voices from South Africa's Township Wars, 1990–4', *African Affairs*, 112 (2013), pp. 283–303.

14 Frankel, p. 483.

15 Etienne Marais, 'Policing the Periphery: Police and Society in South Africa's "homelands"', in *22nd Congress of the South African Sociological Association* (Pretoria, 1992).

16 Gastrow and Shaw, p. 262.

17 Leggett, 'Just Another Miracle', p. 587.

18 Frankel, p. 481.

19 Louw, p. 141.

20 Ted Leggett, 'Improved Crime Reporting: Is South Africa's Crime Wave a Statistical Illusion?', *South African Crime Quarterly*, 1 (2002).

21 Leggett, 'Just Another Miracle', p. 584.

22 Mark Shaw, Jan Van Dijk and Wolfgang Rhomberg, 'Determining Trends in Global Crime and Justice: An Overview of Results from the United Nations Surveys of Crime Trends and Operations of Criminal Justice Systems', *Forum on Crime and Society*, 3 (2003), pp. 35–63 (p. 61).

23 Shaw, Dijk and Rhomberg, p. 61.

24 Asghar Adelzadeh and others, *South Africa Human Development Report 2003*, 2003.

25 Pauline M Wambua, *Call the Police? Across Africa, Citizens Point to Police and Government Performance Issues on Crime*, 2015, p. 7.

26 Dimitri Sanga, Bakary Dosso and Steve Gui-Diby, 'Tracking Progress towards Statistical Capacity Building Efforts: The African Statistical Development Index', *International Statistical Review*, 79 (2011), pp. 303–29 (p. 315).

27 South African Police Service, 'Statement by the Minister for Safety and Security Mr SV Tshwete', 31 May 2001. Available at www.polity.org.za/polity/govdocs/pr/2001/pr0531c.html. Accessed 26 February 2016.

28 Louise Flanagan and Gabi Falanga, 'Police Are Undercounting Murder', *The Star*, 23 September 2015. Available at www.iol.co.za. Accessed 22 January 2016.

29 Chandré Gould, Johan Burger and Gareth Newham, 'The SAPS Crime Statistics: What They Tell Us – and What They Don't', *South African Crime Quarterly*, 42 (2012), p. 4.

30 James O Beasley, 'Serial Murder in America: Case Studies of Seven Offenders', *Behavioral Sciences and the Law*, 22 (2004), pp. 395–414.

31 Brin Hodgskiss, 'Lessons from Serial Murder in South Africa', *Journal of Investigative Psychology and Offender Profiling*, 1 (2004), pp. 67–94 (p. 68).

32 Gérard N Labuschagne and C Gabrielle Salfati, 'An Examination of Serial Homicide in South Africa: The Practice to Research Link', *Journal of Investigative Psychology and Offender Profiling*, 12 (2015), pp. 4–17 (p. 4).

33 Federal Bureau of Investigation, 'Serial Murders: Multi-Disciplinary Perspectives for Investigators', National Center for the Analysis of Violent Crime (NCAVC), US Department of Justice, 2008, 71 (p. 1).

34 Jané Joubert and others, 'Evaluating the Quality of National Mortality

Statistics from Civil Registration in South Africa, 1997-2007', *PloS One*, 8 (2013), e64592 (p. 1).

35 Richard Matzopoulos, Kavi Bhalla and James E Harrison, 'Homicide', in *Oxford Textbook of Violence Prevention: Epidemiology, Evidence, and Policy*, ed. by Peter D Donnelly and Catherine L Ward (Oxford: Oxford University Press, 2015), p. 12.

36 Statistics South Africa, *Mortality and Causes of Death in South Africa, 2014: Findings from Death Notification*, 2015, p. 5.

37 Statistics South Africa, *Mortality and Causes of Death in South Africa, 2014: Findings from Death Notification*, p. 22.

38 Statistics South Africa, *Mortality and Causes of Death in South Africa, 2014: Findings from Death Notification*, p. 42.

39 Richard Matzopoulos, 'Violent Deaths in SA: The 2003 National Injury Mortality Surveillance System', *South African Crime Quarterly*, 2005, pp. 29–36 (p. 34).

40 Antony Altbeker, 'The Dangers of Data: Recognising the Limitations of Crime Statistics', *South African Crime Quarterly*, 2005, pp. 29–36 (p. 29).

41 Rosana Norman and others, 'Are the Cause of Death Statistics Reliable?', 16 February 2005. Available at www.mrc.ac.za. Accessed 18 January 2016.

42 R Matzopoulos and others, 'Injury-Related Mortality in South Africa: A Retrospective Descriptive Study of Postmortem Investigations', *Bulletin of the World Health Organization*, 2015, pp. 1–20 (p. 307).

43 Debbie Bradshaw and others, *Cause of Death Statistics for South Africa: Challenges and Possibilities for Improvement* (South African Medical Research Council, 2010), p. 1. Available at www.mrc.ac.za. Accessed 18 January 2016.

44 R Matzopoulos and others, p. 303.

45 Richard Matzopoulos and others, *The Injury Mortality Survey: A National Study of Injury Mortality Levels and Causes in South Africa in 2009*, 2013, p. 18.

46 Statistics South Africa, *Mortality and Causes of Death in South Africa, 2009: Findings from Death Notification*, 2011, p. 43.

47 Gould, Burger and Newham, p. 4.

48 M Prinsloo and others, 'Validating Homicide Rates in the Western Cape Province, South Africa: Findings from the 2009 Injury Mortality Survey', *South African Medical Journal*, 106 (2016), p. 193.

49 Western Cape Department of Community Safety, *Shadow Report on Safety Information: Murders in the Western Cape: A Case Study*, 2013, p. 5.

50 See Flanagan and Falanga.

51 Medical Research Council & University of South Africa, *A Profile of Fatal Injuries in Mpumalanga 2011*, 2013, p. 5.

52 Antony Altbeker, 'Murder and Robbery in South Africa: A Tale of Two Trends', *Crime, Violence and Injury Prevention in South Africa: Data to Action*, 2008, pp. 131–60.

53 De Kock, Kriegler and Shaw, p. 43.

54 Statistics South Africa, *Victims of Crime Survey 2014/2015*, p. 62.

55 Statistics South Africa, *Victims of Crime Survey 2014/2015*, p. 60.

56 George D Gaskell, Daniel B Wright and Colm A O'Muircheartaigh,

'Telescoping of Landmark Events: Implications for Survey Research', *The Public Opinion Quarterly*, 64 (2000), pp. 77–89.

57 AJ Christopher, 'The Union of South Africa Censuses 1911–1960: An Incomplete Record', *Historia*, 56 (2011), pp. 1–18 (p. 3).

58 Christopher, 'The Union of South Africa Censuses 1911–1960'.

59 Institute for Security Studies, 'ISS Statement: Miscalculations in the 2013 National Crime Ratios', 20 September 2013. Available at www.issafrica. org. Accessed 14 January 2016.

60 Gareth Newham, 'The Police's Serious Crime Statistics Bungle – ISS', Politicsweb, 6 November 2013. Available at www.politicsweb.co.za. Accessed 14 January 2016.

61 South African Police Service, *Annual Report 2014/2015*, p. 200.

62 South African Police Service, *An Analysis of the National Crime Statistics: Addendum to the Annual Report 2013/14*, 2014, p. 38.

63 De Kock, Kriegler and Shaw, p. 38.

64 South African Police Service, *Annual Report 2007/08*, 2008, p. 18.

65 South African Police Service, *An Analysis of the National Crime Statistics: Addendum to the Annual Report 2013/14*, p. 32.

66 South African Police Service, *An Analysis of the National Crime Statistics: Addendum to the Annual Report 2013/14*, p. 45.

67 South African Police Service, *An Analysis of the National Crime Statistics: Addendum to the Annual Report 2013/14*, p. 45.

68 South African Police Service, *Annual Report 2007/08*, p. 21.

69 Smythe, p. 8.

3 Headline international comparison

1 Van Dijk, p. 14.

2 Institute for Economics and Peace, *Global Peace Index 2015: Measuring Peace, Its Causes and Its Economic Value*, 2015, pp. 68–69. Available at www.economicsandpeace.org. Accessed 29 March 2016.

3 Institute for Economics and Peace, p. 9.

4 United Nations Office on Drugs and Crime, *Global Study on Homicide 2013* (Vienna, 2013), p. 16.

5 United Nations Office on Drugs and Crime, p. 9.

6 Statistics South Africa, *Mid-Year Population Estimates 2014*, 2014.

7 Steven Pinker, *The Better Angels of Our Nature: The Decline of Violence in History and Its Causes* (London: Allen Lane, 2011).

8 Aebi, Killias and Tavares, p. 23.

9 Janet P Stamatel, 'An Overview of Publicly Available Quantitative Cross-National Crime Data', *IASSIST Quarterly*, 30 (2006), pp. 16–20 (p. 16).

10 United Nations Office on Drugs and Crime, pp. 12, 22.

11 United Nations Office on Drugs and Crime, p. 11.

12 Altbeker, 'Puzzling Statistics: Is South Africa Really the World's Crime Capital?', p. 2.

13 United Nations Office on Drugs and Crime, pp. 109–110.

14 United Nations Office on Drugs and Crime, pp. 110–111.

15 United Nations Office on Drugs and Crime, p. 102.

16 United Nations Office on Drugs and Crime, pp. 103–108.

17 United Nations Office on Drugs and Crime, p. 23.

18 United Nations Office on Drugs and Crime, UNODC Statistics. Available at data.unodc.org/. Accessed 6 February 2016. South Africa's murder rate has been updated according to the SAPS release for 2014/2015.

19 Renata Giannini, Robert Muggah and Katherine Aguirre, 'It's Really Hard to Say Which City Is the World's Most Murderous', *Global Post*, 27 February 2016. Available at www.globalpost.com. Accessed 29 March 2016.

20 A Lysova and N Shchitov, 'What Is Russia's Real Homicide Rate? Statistical Reconstruction and the "Decivilizing Process"', *Theoretical Criminology*, 19 (2015), pp. 257–77.

21 D Eckberg, 'Trends in Conflict: Uniform Crime Reports, the National Crime Victimization Surveys, and the Lethality of Violent Crime', *Homicide Studies*, 19 (2015), pp. 58–87.

22 Stamatel, p. 16.

23 Aebi, Killias and Tavares, p. 22.

24 World Bank data and statistics, 'Country Groups', 2011. Available at econ. worldbank.org. Accessed 29 March 2016.

25 World Bank, 'Gini Index (World Bank estimate)', 2016. Available at data. worldbank.org/indicator/SI.POV.GINI. Accessed 29 March 2016.

26 Institute for Economics and Peace, p. 32.

27 Amy E Nivette, 'Cross-National Predictors of Crime: A Meta-Analysis', *Homicide Studies*, 15 (2011), pp. 103–31.

28 William Alex Pridemore, 'Poverty Matters: A Reassessment of the Inequality-Homicide Relationship in Cross-National Studies', *British Journal of Criminology*, 51 (2011), pp. 739–72; Marc Ouimet, 'A World of Homicides: The Effect of Economic Development, Income Inequality, and Excess Infant Mortality on the Homicide Rate for 165 Countries in 2010', *Homicide Studies*, 16 (2012), pp. 238–58.

29 Morgan Kelly, 'Inequality and Crime', *Review of Economics and Statistics*, 82 (2000), pp. 530–39 (p. 530).

30 Richard Wilkinson, 'Why Is Violence More Common Where Inequality Is Greater?', *Annals of the New York Academy of Sciences*, 1036 (2004), pp. 1–12 (pp. 2–3).

31 DL Hicks and JH Hicks, 'Jealous of the Joneses: Conspicuous Consumption, Inequality, and Crime', *Oxford Economic Papers*, 66 (2014), pp. 1090–1120.

32 Judith R Blau and Peter M Blau, 'The Cost of Inequality: Metropolitan Structure and Violent Crime', *American Sociological Review*, 47 (1982), pp. 114–29.

33 Ouimet, p. 252.

34 Jeffrey A Miron, 'Violence, Guns, and Drugs: A Cross-Country Analysis', *The Journal of Law & Economics*, 44 (2001), pp. 615–33.

35 Pablo Fajnzylber and others, 'Crime and Victimization: An Economic Perspective', *Economía*, 1 (2014), pp. 219–302.

36 Robert J Sampson and J Robert, 'The Neighborhood Context of Well-Being',

Perspectives in Biology and Medicine, 46 (2003), pp. S53–64.

37 Antony Altbeker, 'Adding Injury to Insult: How Exclusion and Inequality Drive South Africa's Problem of Violence', report on Component 4 of a study conducted by the Centre for the Study of Violence and Reconciliation (CSVR) for the Justice, Crime Prevention and Security (JCPS) cluster, 31 October 2008, p. 4.

38 Gary LaFree and A Tseloni, 'Democracy and Crime: A Multilevel Analysis of Homicide Trends in Forty-Four Countries, 1950-2000', *The ANNALS of the American Academy of Political and Social Science*, 605 (2006), pp. 25–49.

39 Ted Goertzel and others, 'Homicide Booms and Busts: A Small-N Comparative Historical Study', *Homicide Studies*, 17 (2012), p. 70.

40 Amy E Nivette and Manuel Eisner, 'Do Legitimate Polities Have Fewer Homicides? A Cross-National Analysis', *Homicide Studies*, 17 (2013).

41 Nivette and Eisner.

42 Jenny Pearce, 'Perverse State Formation and Securitized Democracy in Latin America', *Democratization*, 17 (2010), pp. 286–306 (p. 288).

43 Jerome L Neapolitan, 'A Comparative Analysis of Nations with Low and High Levels of Violent Crime', *Journal of Criminal Justice*, 27 (1999), pp. 259–74 (p. 263).

44 Eric Neumayer, 'Inequality and Violent Crime: Evidence from Data on Robbery and Violent Theft', *Journal of Peace Research*, 42 (2005), pp. 101–12.

45 World Bank, 'Gini Index (World Bank estimate)'.

46 Michelle Adato, Michael R Carter and Julian May, 'Exploring Poverty Traps and Social Exclusion in South Africa Using Qualitative and Quantitative Data', *Journal of Development Studies*, 42 (2006), pp. 226–47 (p. 226).

47 Murray Leibbrandt and others, 'Trends in South African Income Distribution and Poverty since the Fall of Apartheid', *OECD Social, Employment and Migration Working Papers*, 2010, pp. 1–91.

48 Jeremy Seekings, 'The Continuing Salience of Race: Discrimination and Diversity in South Africa', *Journal of Contemporary African Studies*, 26 (2008), pp. 1–25.

49 Ouimet, p. 252.

50 P Kok and M Collinson, *Migration and Urbanisation in South Africa – Report No. 03-04-02* (Pretoria, 2006), p. 21; Ivan Turok, *Urbanisation and Development in South Africa: Economic Imperatives, Spatial Distortions and Strategic Responses* (Urbanization and emerging population issues, working paper 8, 2012), p. 3.

51 Gary Kynoch, 'Urban Violence in Colonial Africa: A Case for South African Exceptionalism', *Journal of Southern African Studies*, 34 (2008), pp. 629–45.

52 The provenance and context of this quote are disputed.

53 Goertzel and others, p. 67; Bill Dixon, 'The Aetiological Crisis in South African Criminology', *Australian and New Zealand Journal of Criminology*, 46 (2013), pp. 319–34.

54 See, for example, The Centre for the Study of Violence and Reconciliation, *The Violent Nature of Crime in South Africa*, 2007; The Centre for the

Study of Violence and Reconciliation, *Why South Africa Is so Violent and What We Should Be Doing about It*, 2010, xxvii. Available at www.csvr.org.za. Accessed 29 March 2016.

55 UNODC data. Accessed 3 March 2016.

56 UNODC data. Accessed 3 March 2016.

57 Statistics South Africa, *Victims of Crime Survey 2014/2015*, p. 62.

58 Jan van Dijk, John van Kesteren and Paul Smit, *Criminal Victimisation in International Perspective: Key Findings From the 2004–2005 ICVS and EU ICS* (The Hague: Ministry of Justice, WODC, 2007), p. 17. Available at www.unicri.us. Accessed 29 March 2016.

59 Van Dijk, Van Kesteren and Smit, pp. 67, 73.

60 Ugljesa Zvecic and Anna Alvazzi del Frate, 'Experiences of Victimisation', in *Victims of Crime in the Developing World* (Rome: United Nations, 1998), pp. 29–59 (pp. 30–31).

61 John van Kesteren, Pat Mayhew and Paul Nieuwbeerta, *Criminal Victimisation in Seventeen Industrialised Countries: Key Findings from the 2000 International Crime Victim Survey* (The Hague: Ministry of Justice, WODC), p. 74.

62 Van Kesteren, Mayhew and Nieuwbeerta, p. 65.

63 Statistics South Africa, *Victims of Crime Survey 2014/2015*, p. 62.

64 Jennifer L Truman and Lynn Langton, *Criminal Victimization, 2014*, 2015, p. 3.

65 John Flatley, *Crime in England and Wales, Year Ending March 2015*, 2015, p. Table 11B. Available at www.ons.gov.uk/ons/dcp171778_371127.pdf. Accessed 29 March 2016.

66 Wambua, p. 5.

67 Wambua, p. 4.

68 UNODC data. Accessed 6 February 2016.

4 Breaking down the numbers

1 Silber and Geffen.

2 Statistics South Africa, *Census 2011 Metadata*, 2012, pp. 9–10.

3 Federal Bureau of Investigation, 'Uniform Crime Reports 2014: Crime in the United States'. Available at www.fbi.gov. Accessed 3 March 2016.

4 Edward L Glaeser and Bruce Sacerdote, 'Why Is There More Crime in Cities?', *Journal of Political Economy*, 107 (1999), pp. S225–58.

5 United Nations Office on Drugs and Crime, p. 12.

6 Assistance in this was kindly granted by the University of Cape Town's GIS Laboratory.

7 Available for download at: www.statssa.gov.za/?page_id=1854&PPN=P0302&SCH=6334.

8 R Wortley and L Mazerolle, 'Environmental Criminology and Crime Analysis', in *Crime Science Series*, 2008, p. 294 (p. 4).

9 Alessandra Heinemann and Dorte Verner, 'Crime and Violence in Development: A Literature Review of Latin America and the Caribbean',

World Bank Policy Research Working Paper 4041, 2006, pp. 1–26 (p. 3).

10 An incomplete list is available at data.unodc.org. Accessed 3 March 2016.

11 Federal Bureau of Investigation, 'Uniform Crime Reports 2014'.

12 Federal Bureau of Investigation, 'Uniform Crime Reports 2014'.

13 See, for example, Jeremy Seekings, *Economy, Society and Municipal Services in Khayelitsha*, 2013, p. 2.

14 Commission of Inquiry into Allegations of Police Inefficiency and a Breakdown in Relations between SAPS and the Community in Khayelitsha, p. 37.

15 South African Police Service, *An Analysis of the National Crime Statistics: Addendum to the Annual Report 2011/2012*, 2012, p. 53.

16 Heike Goudriaan, Karin Wittebrood and Paul Nieuwbeerta, 'Neighbourhood Characteristics and Reporting Crime: Effects of Social Cohesion, Confidence in Police Effectiveness and Socio-Economic Disadvantage', *British Journal of Criminology*, 46 (2006), pp. 719–42; Wesley G Skogan, 'Citizen Reporting of Crime', *Criminology*, 13 (1976), pp. 535–49.

17 Sara K Thompson and Rosemary Gartner, 'The Spatial Distribution and Social Context of Homicide in Toronto's Neighborhoods', *Journal of Research in Crime and Delinquency*, 2014, LI, p. 89.

18 Thompson and Gartner.

19 Paul Nieuwbeerta and others, 'Neighborhood Characteristics and Individual Homicide Rates: Effects of Social Cohesion, Confidence in the Police, and Socioeconomic Disadvantage', *Homicide Studies*, 12 (2008), pp. 90–116.

20 Patricia L Mccall and Paul Nieuwbeerta, 'Structural Covariates of Homicide Rates: A European City Cross-National Comparative Analysis', *Homicide Studies*, 11 (2007), pp. 167–88.

21 Alex Sutherland, Ian Brunton-Smith and Jonathan Jackson, 'Collective Efficacy, Deprivation and Violence in London', *British Journal of Criminology*, 53 (2013), pp. 1050–74.

22 Robert J Sampson and Per-Olof H Wikström, 'The Social Order of Violence in Chicago and Stockholm Neighbourhoods: A Comparative Inquiry', in *Order, Conflict and Violence*, ed. by SN Kalyva, I Shapiro and T Masoud (Cambridge University Press, 2008).

23 R Barata and M Ribeiro, 'Intra-Urban Differentials in Death Rates From Homicide in the City of São Paulo, Brazil, 1988–1994', *Social Science & Medicine*, 47 (1998), pp. 19–23; Vânia Ceccato, Robert Haining and Tulio Kahn, 'The Geography of Homicide in São Paulo, Brazil', *Environment and Planning A*, 39 (2007), pp. 1632–53.

24 Célia Landmann Szwarcwald and others, 'Income Inequality and Homicide Rates in Rio de Janeiro, Brazil', *American Journal of Public Health*, 89 (1999), pp. 845–50.

25 Patrice K Morris and Adam Graycar, 'Homicide through a Different Lens', *British Journal of Criminology*, 51 (2011), pp. 823–38.

26 Lance E. Hannon, 'Extremely Poor Neighborhoods and Homicide', *Social Science Quarterly*, 86 (2005), pp. 1418–34; RD Peterson and LJ Krivo, 'Segregated Spatial Locations, Race-Ethnic Composition, and Neighborhood Violent Crime', *The ANNALS of the American Academy of*

Political and Social Science, 623 (2009), pp. 93–107.

27 Robert D Baller and others, 'Structural Covariates of US Country Homicide Rates: Incorporating Spatial Effects', *Criminology*, 39 (2001), pp. 561–90 (p. 562).

28 Robert J Kane, 'Compromised Police Legitimacy as a Predictor of Violent Crime in Structurally Disadvantaged Communities', *Criminology*, 43 (2005), pp. 469–98. David S Kirk and Andrew V Papachristos, 'Cultural Mechanisms and the Persistence of Neighborhood Violence', *American Journal of Sociology*, 116 (2011), pp. 1190–1233.

29 Peterson and Krivo.

30 Jeffrey D Morenoff, Robert J Sampson and Stephen W Raudenbush, 'Neighbourhood Inequality, Collective Efficacy, and the Spatial Dynamics of Urban Violence', *Criminology*, 39 (2001), pp. 517–60; Ching-Chi Hsieh and MD Pugh, 'Poverty, Income Inequality, and Violent Cime: A Meta-Analysis of Recent Aggregate Data Studies', *Criminal Justice Review*, 18 (1993), pp. 182–202.

31 Steven D Levitt, 'The Changing Relationship between Income and Crime Victimization', *Economic Policy Review*, 5 (1999), pp. 87–98 (p. 87).

32 Alejandro Gaviria and Carmen Pagés, 'Patterns of Crime Victimization in Latin American Cities', *Journal of Development Economics*, 67 (2002), pp. 181–203.

33 Tim Hope, 'The Distribution of Household Property Crime Victimisation: Insights from the British Crime Survey', in *Surveying Crime in the 21st Century*, ed. by MG Maxfield and M Hough, Crime Prev (New York: Criminal Justice Press, 2007).

34 Alejandro Gaviria and Carlos Eduardo Vélez, 'Who Bears the Burden of Crime in Colombia?', *SSRN Electronic Journal*, 2001.

35 Rafael di Tella, Sebastian Galiani and Ernesto Schargrodsky, *Crime Victimization and Income Distribution*, 2002.

36 Van Kesteren, Mayhew and Nieuwbeerta, p. 54.

37 Anders Nilsson and Felipe Estrada, 'The Inequality of Victimization: Trends in Exposure to Crime among Rich and Poor', *European Journal of Criminology*, 3 (2006), pp. 387–412 (p. 389).

38 Giannini, Muggah and Aguirre.

39 Wazimap, 'Ward 61 (79800061)'. Available at wazimap.co.za/profiles/ward-79800061/. Accessed 29 March 2016.

40 Statistics South Africa, *Victims of Crime Survey 2014/2015*, p. 75.

41 Valerie Møller, 'Resilient or Resigned? Criminal Victimisation and Quality of Life in South Africa', *Social Indicators Research*, 72 (2005), pp. 263–317 (p. 267).

42 Nahla Valji, Bronwyn Harris and Graeme Simpson, 'Crime, Security and Fear of the Other', *SA Reconciliation Barometer*, 2 (2004).

43 The Centre for the Study of Violence and Reconciliation, *The Violent Nature of Crime in South Africa*, p. 65.

44 Statistics South Africa, *Victims of Crime Survey 2014/2015*, pp. 92, 94.

45 Statistics South Africa, *Victims of Crime Survey 2014/2015*, pp. 92, 94.

46 Statistics South Africa, *Victims of Crime Survey 2011/2012*, pp. 65, 67; Statistics South Africa, *Victims of Crime Survey 2013/2014* (Pretoria, 2014),

pp. 73, 75; Statistics South Africa, *Victims of Crime Survey 2014/2015*, pp. 92, 94.

47 Statistics South Africa, *Victims of Crime Survey 2014/2015*, pp. 92, 94.

48 Statistics South Africa data portal at interactive.statssa.gov.za:8282/ webview/, see Victims of Crime Survey > 2014_2015 > selected person > Population group of household members, Experience of individual crime, and Robbery – were you injured, weighted tabulations. Accessed 31 March 2016.

49 Statistics South Africa data portal at interactive.statssa.gov.za:8282/ webview/, see Victims of Crime Survey > 2014_2015 > household > Population group of the persons in the household, housebreaking/ burglary – reporting crime to the police, weighted tabulations. Accessed 31 March 2016.

50 JDS Thomson, 'Coloured Homicide Trends in South Africa', *South African Crime Quarterly*, 2004, pp. 9–14 (p. 10); R Matzopoulos and others, p. 307.

51 R Matzopoulos and others, p. 310.

52 Altbeker, 'Puzzling Statistics', p. 6.

53 Daniel Kay Hertz, 'Homicide Inequality in Chicago – in Maps', *New Republic*, 9 June 2014. Available at newrepublic.com. Accessed 29 March 2016.

54 Lawrence W Sherman, 'Hot Spots of Crime and Criminal Careers of Places', *Crime and Place*, 4 (1995), pp. 35–52 (p. 86).

55 Alexandra Hiropoulos and Jeremy Porter, 'Visualising Property Crime in Gauteng: Applying GIS to Crime Pattern Theory', *South African Crime Quarterly*, 2014.

56 Violence and Injury Lead Programme MRC/UNISA Crime, *A Profile of Fatal Injuries in South Africa*, 2008.

57 Gregory D Breetzke and Ellen G Cohn, 'Seasonal Assault and Neighborhood Deprivation in South Africa: Some Preliminary Findings', *Environment and Behavior*, 44 (2012), pp. 641–67.

58 South African Police Service, *Annual Report 2014/2015*, p. 199.

59 South African Police Service, *Annual Report 2014/2015*, p. 234.

60 Commission of Inquiry into Allegations of Police Inefficiency and a Breakdown in Relations between SAPS and the Community in Khayelitsha, p. 314.

61 South African Police Service, *Annual Report 2014/2015*, p. 209.

62 Robyn Pharoah, *The Dynamics of Crime: Comparing the Results from the 1998, 2003 and 2007 National Crime and Victimisation Surveys*, 2008, p. 9.

63 Naeemah Abrahams and others, 'Intimate Partner Femicide in South Africa in 1999 and 2009', *PLoS Medicine*, 10 (2013), p. 3.

64 MRC/UNISA Crime.

65 R Matzopoulos and others, p. 308.

66 Pablo Fajnzylber, Daniel Lederman, Norman Loayza, Peter Reuter, John Roman and Alejandro Gaviria, 'Crime and Victimization: An Economic Perspective', *Economía*, 1 (2014), 219–302, p. 11.

67 David Thacher, 'The Rich Get Richer and the Poor Get Robbed: Inequality in US Criminal Victimization, 1974–2000', *Journal of Quantitative Criminology*, 20 (2004), pp. 89–116; Shaw, Tunstall and Dorling.

68 The SAPS currently releases its figures in Excel format around mid-September each year, on its website (www.saps.gov.za). The Institute for Security Studies presents these in a range of useful formats on its website (www.issafrica.org/crimehub/).
69 Megan Govender, 'The Paradox of Crime Perceptions: SAPS Crime Statistics, Victims of Crime Surveys and the Media', *South African Crime Quarterly*, 2013.

5 A national history of murder, 1911–2015

1 Department of Police, Union of South Africa, *Annual Departmental Report, 1920–1921*, p. 68.
2 Population Division United Nations, Department of Economic and Social Affairs, 'World Population Prospects: The 2015 Revision', 2015. Available at esa.un.org. Accessed 23 January 2016.
3 United Nations Office on Drugs and Crime, pp. 12, 22.
4 Kynoch, 'Urban Violence in Colonial Africa: A Case for South African Exceptionalism', p. 631.
5 Department of Police, Union of South Africa, *Annual Departmental Report, 1925–1926*, pp. 80–81.
6 Clive Glaser, 'Violent Crime in South Africa: Historical Perspectives', *South African Historical Journal*, 60 (2008), pp. 334–52 (p. 340).
7 Mark Shaw, *Crime and Policing in Post-Apartheid South Africa: Transforming under Fire* (Cape Town: David Philip Publishers, 2002), p. 2.
8 Williamson, pp. 185, 186.
9 'SA Crime-Busters in Action', *Rand Daily Mail*, 17 August 1979.
10 'When Violence Becomes a Way of Life …', *Rand Daily Mail*, 12 June 1979.
11 'SA Has Second Highest Murder Rate', *Pretoria News*, 30 August 1983.
12 'Vlok Warns of "a Nation of Gangsters"', *The Cape Times*, 28 January 1991.
13 SAP annual reports and South African Institute of Race Relations, *Race Relations Survey 1993/1994* (Johannesburg: South African Institute of Race Relations, 1994).
14 'When Violence Becomes a Way of Life …'
15 Turok, p. 3.
16 William Beinart, 'Introduction: Political and Collective Violence in Southern African Historiography', *Journal of Southern African Studies*, 18 (1992), pp. 455–86 (pp. 465–468).
17 Shaw, p. 10.
18 Shaw, p. 12.
19 Super, p. 4.
20 Super, p. 5.
21 South African Institute of Race Relations, *Race Relations Survey*, various years (Johannesburg: South African Institute of Race Relations).
22 South African Police, *Annual Report 1993*, p. 103.
23 Neapolitan, p. 270.
24 Leggett, 'Just Another Miracle', p. 582.

25 Statistics South Africa, *Victims of Crime Survey 1998*, 1999, p. 120.
26 Statistics South Africa, *Victims of Crime Survey 1998*, p. 14.
27 Robyn Pharoah, *National Victims of Crime Survey: Overview of Key Findings*, 2008, p. 4.
28 Statistics South Africa, *Victims of Crime Survey 2014/2015*, p. 60.
29 Gould, Burger and Newham, p. 4.
30 Louw, p. 138.
31 Pinker, p. xxii.
32 Pinker, p. xxii.
33 Glaser, p. 334.
34 Comaroff and Comaroff, pp. 216–217.

6 The changing character of violence, 1994–2015

1 Bruce, "'The Ones in the Pile Were the Ones Going Down'", p. 10.
2 Robert Nash Parker and M Dwayne Smith, 'Deterrence, Poverty, and Type of Homicide', *American Journal of Sociology*, 85 (1979), pp. 614–24.
3 David Bruce, 'Anger, Hatred, or Just Heartlessness? Defining Gratuitous Violence', *South African Crime Quarterly*, 2010, pp. 13–22 (p. 14).
4 Vanessa Barolsky, Nadia Sanger and Catherine L Ward, *Case Studies of Perpetrators of Violent Crime*, 2008, p. 15.
5 Barolsky, Sanger and Ward, p. 15.
6 Ellen G Cohn and James Rotton, 'Even Criminals Take a Holiday: Instrumental and Expressive Crimes on Major and Minor Holidays', *Journal of Criminal Justice*, 31 (2003), pp. 351–60 (p. 358).
7 Charis E Kubrin, 'Structural Covariates Of Homicide Rates: Does Type Of Homicide Matter?', *Journal of Research in Crime and Delinquency*, 40 (2003), pp. 139–70.
8 Sean Patrick Varano and Jeffret Michael Cancino, 'An Empirical Analysis of Deviant Homicides in Chicago', *Homicide Studies*, 5 (2001), pp. 5–29.
9 Scott H Decker, 'Deviant Homicide: A New Look at the Role of Motives and Victim-Offender Relationships', *Journal of Research in Crime and Delinquency*, 33 (1996), pp. 427–49.
10 Liqun Cao, Charles Hou and Bu Huang, 'Correlates of the Victim-Offender Relationship in Homicide', *International Journal of Offender Therapy and Comparative Criminology*, 52 (2008), pp. 658–72 (p. 659).
11 Decker, 'Deviant Homicide'.
12 Charis E Kubrin and Tim Wadsworth, 'Identifying the Structural Correlates of African American Killings: What Can We Learn From Data Disaggregation?', *Homicide Studies*, 7 (2003), pp. 3–35.
13 C Hessick, 'Violence between Lovers, Strangers and Friends', *Washington University Law Review*, 85 (2007), pp. 343–407 (p. 344).
14 Mailie Green, 'Media Representations of Gratuitous Violence in South Africa' (unpublished MA thesis, University of the Witwatersrand, no date), p. 82.
15 Duxita Mistry, Rika Snyman and Marielize van Zyl, *Social Fabric Crime*

in the Northern Cape, ed. by Ron Paschke and Jean Redpath, 2001, pp. 21–22.

16 Johan van Graan and Marcel Van der Watt, 'Case Docket Analysis: An Effective Crime Information Product for Criminal Investigators, Crime Analysts and Crime Researchers', *Acta Criminologica*, 27 (2014), pp. 144–59 (p. 145).

17 Johan Burger, Chandré Gould and Gareth Newham, 'The State of Crime in South Africa: An Analysis of the SAPS Crime Statistics for 2009/10', *South African Crime Quarterly*, 34 (2010), pp. 3–12 (p. 10).

18 The Centre for the Study of Violence and Reconciliation, *Streets of Pain, Streets of Sorrow: The Circumstances of the Occurrence of Murder in Six Areas with High Murder Rates*, 2008, pp. 28, 31.

19 The Centre for the Study of Violence and Reconciliation, *Streets of Pain, Streets of Sorrow*, p. 28.

20 Van Graan and Van der Watt, p. 151.

21 Rika Snyman, *A Profile of the Murder Victim in South Africa as an Aid to Prevention*, ed. by Chris Sumner, Mark Israel, *et al*, *International Victimology: Selected Papers from the 8th International Symposium on Victimology* (Canberra, 1996), p. 314.

22 Chris De Kock, 'No, Mr Nhleko, Murder Is Preventable', Politicsweb, 24 November 2015. Available at www.politicsweb.co.za. Accessed 29 March 2016.

23 Shaw, p. 54.

24 South African Police Service, *Annual Report 2009/10*, 2010, p. 9.

25 Leah Gilbert, 'Urban Violence and Health – South Africa 1995', *Social Science & Medicine*, 43 (1996), pp. 873–86 (p. 881).

26 South African Police Service, *Annual Report 2008/09*, 2009, p. 10.

27 Leggett, 'The Sieve Effect', p. 12.

28 SAPS, *Detective Services 2007/2008*, 2008, p. 115.

29 De Kock, 'No, Mr Nhleko, Murder Is Preventable'.

30 South African Police Service, *Annual Performance Plan 2010/2011*, p. 32.

31 The Centre for the Study of Violence and Reconciliation, *The Violent Nature of Crime in South Africa*, p. 186.

32 Statistics South Africa, *Victims of Crime Survey 1997 – Full*, 1998, p. 47.

33 SAPS Strategic Managment, *Analysis of the National Crime Statistics 2013/2014*, 2014, p. 79.

34 SAPS Strategic Managment, *Analysis of the National Crime Statistics 2013/2014*, p. 79.

35 Bruce, '"The Ones in the Pile Were the Ones Going Down"'.

36 Statistics South Africa, *Victims of Crime Survey 1997 – Full*, pp. iv, v.

37 Patrick Burton and others, *National Victims of Crime Survey South Africa 2003*, 2004, p. 103.

38 Burton and others, p. 18.

39 Burton and others, p. 107.

40 Pharoah, *The Dynamics of Crime: Comparing the Results from the 1998, 2003 and 2007 National Crime and Victimisation Surveys*, pp. 1, 9.

41 Statistics South Africa, *Victims of Crime Survey 2011*, p. 39.

42 Smythe.

43 Jewkes and Abrahams, p. 1232.
44 Statistics South Africa, *Victims of Crime Survey 2014/2015*, p. 62.
45 Statistics South Africa, *Victims of Crime Survey 2014/2015*, p. 79.
46 Statistics South Africa, *Victims of Crime Survey 1997 – Full*, p. 47.
47 Statistics South Africa, *Victims of Crime Survey 2014/2015*, p. 76.
48 Pharoah, *The Dynamics of Crime*, p. 9.
49 Burton and others, p. 128.
50 Statistics South Africa data portal at interactive.statssa.gov.za:8282/
   webview/, see Victims of Crime Survey > 2014_2015 > selected person
   > assault – injuries sustained and medical attention needed, weighted
   tabulations. Accessed 31 March 2016.
51 Gilbert, p. 877.
52 Richard G Matzopoulos, Mary Lou Thompson and Jonathan E Myers,
   'Firearm and Nonfirearm Homicide in 5 South African Cities: A
   Retrospective Population-Based Study', *American Journal of Public
   Health*, 104 (2014), pp. 455–60 (p. 455).
53 Matzopoulos, Thompson and Myers, p. 455.
54 Matzopoulos, Thompson and Myers, p. 457.
55 Matzopoulos, Thompson and Myers.
56 Hessick, p. 362.
57 Scott H Decker, 'Exploring Victim-Offender Relationships in Homicide:
   The Role of Individual and Event Characteristics', *Justice Quarterly*, 10
   (1993), pp. 585–612 (p. 587).
58 Bruce, '"The Ones in the Pile Were the Ones Going Down"', p. 10.
59 Statistics South Africa, *Victims of Crime Survey 2014/2015*, p. 75.
60 Statistics South Africa, *Victims of Crime Survey 1998*, p. 28.
61 Statistics South Africa, *Victims of Crime Survey 1998*, p. 127.
62 Pharoah, *The Dynamics of Crime: Comparing the Results from the 1998,
   2003 and 2007 National Crime and Victimisation Surveys*, p. 1. Statistics
   South Africa, *Victims of Crime Survey 2011*, p. 38. Statistics South Africa,
   Victims of Crime Survey 2014/2015, p. 62.
63 Statistics South Africa, *Victims of Crime Survey 2014/2015*, p. 62.
64 Altbeker, 'Murder and Robbery in South Africa'.
65 The Centre for the Study of Violence and Reconciliation, *Streets of Pain,
   Streets of Sorrow*, p. 12,13.
66 SAPS Strategic Managment, *Analysis of the National Crime Statistics
   2013/2014*, 2014, p. 12.
67 South African Police Service, *An Analysis of the National Crime Statistics:
   Addendum to the Annual Report 2011/2012*, p. 44.
68 South African Police Service, *Annual Report 2007/08*, p. 16.
69 South African Banking Risk Information Centre, 'Industry Pleased by
   Decrease in Associated Robberies', 2015 Available at www.sabric.co.za.
   Accessed 28 January 2016.
70 Statistics South Africa, *Victims of Crime Survey 2014/2015*, p. 62.
71 Barbara Holtmann and Carmen Domingo-Swarts, 'Current Trends and
   Responses to Crime in South Africa', in *Crime, Violence and Injury
   Prevention in South Africa: Data to Action*, ed. by Ashley van Niekerk and
   Shahnaaz Suffla, 2008, pp. 97–121 (p. 110).

72 Jenni Irish and Kevin Qhobosheane, *South Africa, Penetrating State and Business: Organised Crime in Southern Africa*, ISS Monograph 89, 1 October 2003, pp. 104–105.

73 'Zero Tolerance for Criminals', City of Johannesburg News, 2011. Available at www.joburg.org.za. Accessed 26 January 2016.

74 SAPS Strategic Managment, *Analysis of the National Crime Statistics 2013/2014*, p. 11.

75 De Kock, Kriegler and Shaw, pp. 31–32.

76 David Bruce, 'Focus on "Trio" Crimes Skews the Stats', *Mail & Guardian*, 3 October 2014. Available at mg.co.za. Accessed 29 March 2016.

77 De Kock, Kriegler and Shaw, p. 27.

78 Statistics South Africa, *Victims of Crime Survey 2014/2015*, p. 8.

79 SAPS Strategic Management, *Analysis of the National Crime Statistics 2013/2014*, p. 11.

80 Martin Innes, *Signal Crime: Social Reactions to Crime, Disorder, and Control* (Oxford: Oxford University Press, 2014).

81 South African Police Service, *Annual Report 2007/08*, p. 21.

82 Pharoah, *National Victims of Crime Survey: Overview of Key Findings*, p. 4.

83 Pharoah, *National Victims of Crime Survey: Overview of Key Findings*, p. 5.

84 Statistics South Africa, *Victims of Crime Survey 2014/2015*, p. 62.

85 Statistics South Africa, *Victims of Crime Survey 1997 – Full*, p. vi; Burton and others, p. 79.

86 Pharoah, *National Victims of Crime Survey: Overview of Key Findings*, p. 13.

87 Statistics South Africa, *Victims of Crime Survey 2014/2015*, p. 39.

88 William R Pruitt, 'The Progress of Democratic Policing in Post-Apartheid South Africa', *African Journal of Criminology & Justice Studies*, 4 (2010), pp. 116–40.

89 Statistics South Africa, *Victims of Crime Survey 2014/2015*, p. 67.

90 Pharoah, *The Dynamics of Crime: Comparing the Results from the 1998, 2003 and 2007 National Crime and Victimisation Surveys*, p. 8.

91 Statistics South Africa data portal at interactive.statssa.gov.za:8282/ webview/, see Victims of Crime Survey > 2014_2015 > selected person > robbery – do you know the robber, weighted tabulations. Accessed 31 March 2016.

92 Statistics South Africa data portal at interactive.statssa.gov.za:8282/ webview/, see Victims of Crime Survey > 2014_2015 > selected person > robbery – how (do you know the robber), province, weighted tabulations. Accessed 31 March 2016.

93 Varano and Cancino.

Conclusion: what makes crime go down?

1 Statistics South Africa, *National Household Travel Survey*, 2014, p. 7.

2 Statistics South Africa, *Victims of Crime Survey 2014/2015*, p. 62.

3 Statistics South Africa, *Victims of Crime Survey 2014/2015*, p. 62.

4 SAPS Strategic Management, *Analysis of the National Crime Statistics 2013/2014*, p. 37.
5 De Kock, Kriegler and Shaw, p. 37.
6 De Kock, Kriegler and Shaw, p. 37.
7 Josh Barro, 'Here's Why Stealing Cars Went Out of Fashion', *The New York Times*, 11 August 2014. Available at www.nytimes.com. Accessed 29 March 2016.
8 Statistics South Africa, *Victims of Crime Survey 2014/2015*, p. 8.
9 Statistics South Africa, *Victims of Crime Survey 2014/2015*, p. 60.
10 Statistics South Africa, *Victims of Crime Survey 2014/2015*, p. 22.
11 Pharoah, *National Victims of Crime Survey: Overview of Key Findings*, p. 10.
12 Monique Marks and Chris Overall, 'Breaking Down Walls: New Solutions for More Effective Urban Crime Prevention in South African Cities', *Stability: International Journal of Security & Development*, 4 (2015), pp. 1–19.
13 Holtmann and Domingo-Swarts, p. 115.
14 Statistics South Africa, *Victims of Crime Survey 2014/2015*, p. 18.
15 Karl Peltzer and others, 'Illicit Drug Use and Treatment in South Africa: A Review', *Substance Use and Misuse*, 45 (2010), pp. 2221–43.
16 Simon Howell and Katherine Couzyn, 'The South African National Drug Master Plan 2013–2017: A Critical Review', *South African Journal of Criminal Justice*, 28 (2015), pp. 1–23 (p. 2).

Index

Entries in *italics* refer to figures or tables